MIDWAY AND GUADALCANAL

TURNING POINTS OF WAR II

MIDWAY AND GUADAL-CANAL

TOM McGOWEN

A GROLIER COMPANY

FRANKLIN WATTS ■ 1984
NEW YORK ■ LONDON ■ TORONTO ■ SYDNEY

Photographs courtesy of:
The National Archives: pp. 2, 6, 12, 35;
Culver Pictures, Inc.: pp. 5, 46;
Navy Department: pp. 21, 52;
UPI: pp. 42, 49, 69, 74, 78, 84, 95;
U.S. Marine Corps: pp. 62, 66.

Maps courtesy of Vantage Art, Inc.

Library of Congress Cataloging in Publication Data

McGowen, Tom.
Midway and Guadalcanal.

(Turning points of World War II)
Includes index.
Summary: Details the World War II battles between
the Americans and the Japanese at the Pacific islands
of Midway and Guadalcanal.
1. Midway, Battle of, 1942—Juvenile literature.
2. Guadalcanal Island (Solomon Islands), Battle of, 1942-
1943—Juvenile literature. [1. Midway, Battle of, 1942.
2. Guadalcanal Island (Solomon Islands), Battle of, 1942-
1943. 3. World War, 1939-1945—Pacific Ocean]
I. Title. II. Series.
D774.M5M35 1984   940.54'26   84-10398
ISBN 0-531-04866-7

CONTENTS

ESPECIALLY FOR
MY BROTHER, BILL

MIDWAY AND
GUADALCANAL

PROLOGUE

The warships of the U.S. Navy and the empire of Japan, which played such a tremendously important part in the Pacific Ocean fighting in World War II, were quite a bit different from the warships of today. Most of them had no radar, none of them had such things as computers or rocket missiles, and none of them could go for such enormously long periods of time without refueling as today's nuclear-powered ships can. They communicated with each other, with shore bases, and with aircraft, by means of dot and dash codes sent and received by radio. To understand why certain things happened in certain ways at such important battles as the Battle of Midway and the battles fought in the waters around the island of Guadalcanal, it is important to know a little about what the ships and weapons of World War II could and couldn't do.

Today, except for the United States, no major navies make any use of the vessel called a *battleship*, but at the beginning of World War II the battleship was regarded as the most important kind of warship. A battleship was basically just a big floating platform for between eight and sixteen enormous guns that could fire huge shells twenty miles (32 km) or more—about the farthest range possible for a weapon, then. The size of a battleship's guns was indicated by the width of the shells they fired, which might be 14, 16, or 18 inches (36, 41,or 56 cm). Of course, the wider and longer the

The battleship Maryland *is shown here in front of the aircraft carrier* Lexington, *which was lost in the Battle of* ~~Midway.~~

Coral Sea
(may '42)

shell, the bigger the explosion it made. Thus, just one battleship was the equal of a number of smaller ships; it could stay well out of range of their smaller guns and smash them to scrap metal with its big ones. On the other hand, a battleship was so heavily armored, with thick steel plate that could resist many explosions, that it could take a tremendous amount of punishment and still keep fighting. A naval force that included a number of battleships was a force greatly feared by its opponents, while a force with few or no battleships was at a disadvantage. An average American battleship was a bit more than 880 feet (267 m) long and had a crew of about 2,800 men.

A *cruiser* was a kind of small battleship that could move faster, and go farther before needing more fuel, than a battleship could. It was heavily armored and could take a lot of punishment, but its guns were much smaller than those of a battleship. There were two kinds of cruisers, light and heavy, the difference being that a heavy cruiser generally had 8-inch (20 cm) guns while a light cruiser would have 6-inchers (15 cm). A cruiser might also have torpedo tubes for launching torpedoes—self-propelled missiles—into the water, and generally carried from two to four seaplanes (planes that could land in water) which were literally *shot* into the air by means of a mechanical catapult. A couple of heavy cruisers might give a battleship a good fight, and a force of a battleship and a few cruisers could be extremely dangerous. A typical American cruiser was about 600 feet (182 m) long and had a crew of somewhat more than 850.

A World War II *destroyer* was a fairly small, fast ship that could move about and turn quickly, and was used mostly for protecting bigger, slower ships—such as battleships or transports—from submarine attacks. A group of destroyers would form a protective ring or box around the bigger ship and crewmen would keep careful watch for enemy subs. If a sub was seen, or detected by means of listening devices, destroyers could attack it by dropping depth charges, which were large underwater bombs that looked like oil drums.

Destroyers also had torpedo tubes and a number of small guns, and because they were fast and quick-turning they might be able to gang up on a bigger ship and do some damage to it. But a destroyer had no armor and was easily damaged itself. A destroyer might be 370 feet (112 m) long or longer, with a crew of several hundred.

An *aircraft carrier* of World War II, like such a ship today, was essentially a floating airfield. The purpose of an aircraft carrier at the beginning of the war was to provide a fleet of warships with enough planes to make strong bombing and torpedo attacks on enemy fleets while the other ships were attacking the enemy with gunfire. But as time went on, this idea changed, and aircraft carriers became the main part of a fleet instead of just "helpers."

An aircraft carrier consisted basically of two decks: the upper deck was a flat surface on which planes could take off and land, and the deck below was used as a huge hangar where planes could be "tuned up," repaired, and stored. A carrier's top deck, called the flight deck, had two elevator sections that could be raised or lowered so that planes could be taken down to the hangar deck or brought up to the flight deck. As long as a battleship and quite a bit wider, a carrier might have had as many as ninety airplanes and required a crew of several thousand men. Naturally, such a huge, complicated vessel took a long time to build and was tremendously expensive as well as being an essential part of a

This unusual photograph shows the flight deck of an aircraft carrier where crewmen are at work on several torpedo bombers. Other crewmen are taking the elevator down to the hangar deck.

fleet's air power, so every effort was made to protect carriers and try to keep them out of harm's way. They had little armor, and had to depend on a guard of ships, usually cruisers and destroyers, to protect them from enemy vessels. To guard them against hostile planes they had to rely on their antiaircraft guns and those of their guards, as well as their own fighter planes, which in time of danger were kept circling above, ready to attack and shoot down anything that tried to get at the carrier.

A *submarine* of World War II could not launch missiles from underwater up into the air as nuclear submarines can do now; its main purposes were to spy on enemy warship and convoy movements and to sneak in to launch torpedoes at big, slow-moving ships such as aircraft carriers and troop transports. This was not easy to do, as such ships were usually heavily guarded by destroyers that kept watch for enemy subs. A depth charge exploding close to a submarine could break open the hull, letting in water and dooming the ship and its crew.

The U.S. Navy made particular use of little vessels called *PT Boats*, or Patrol Torpedo Boats. A PT Boat was little more than a large motorboat with torpedo tubes and a few small guns, but was extremely fast and quick turning, able to race in at a larger ship such as a destroyer, launch torpedoes, and race away again. But it had no armor and was easily destroyed. A PT Boat was from 70 to 90 feet (21 to 27 m) long and had a top speed of a little more than 55 mph (88 kph).

The ships of World War II all ran on oil and needed frequent big "drinks" of oil to keep going. Oil for ships at sea was provided by *tankers*, or *oilers*, which were literally float-

A World War II submarine rescues combat airmen whose plane went down in the Pacific.

■ 7 ■

ing fuel tanks—huge ships filled with oil. A fleet of warships going any long distance generally had to have a few tankers with it; ships on a steady patrol out at sea would arrange to meet a tanker from time to time in order to refuel.

The numbers of all these kinds of ships that were available to them, and the things that each kind of ship could and couldn't do, affected the plans of both American and Japanese commanders throughout the war in the Pacific. Certain decisions were made simply because there were plenty, or because there weren't enough, of particular kinds of ships. Events during the Battle of Midway and during the struggle for Guadalcanal were often the result of such decisions.

CHAPTER

THE
INVINCIBLE
RISING
SUN

Throughout the Pacific Ocean are scattered many thousands of islands, some no more than tiny piles of rock, and others large masses of land many thousands of square miles in size. During the nineteenth century and early part of the twentieth century, some of the more powerful nations of the world took over many of these islands to use as naval and military bases—places where warships could safely go for needed fuel, supplies, and fresh water, and to make repairs; where troops could be brought together, equipped, armed, and put on ships that would take them where they were needed to fight; and, by the 1930s, where airplanes could take off and land, and be armed and fueled for bombing attacks on enemy ships and bases. Generals, admirals, and politicians of the nations that had bases in the Pacific all knew that if war ever broke out there, it would be fought over the bases. It would be a war in which fleets of warships would be used to protect their own bases and to land troops to take over enemy bases. The side that could inflict the most destruction on the enemy's warships and could take over the most of the enemy's bases would win.

In the year 1941, the United States, the empire of Japan, Great Britain, and the Netherlands all had numbers of bases and possessions throughout the Pacific area. The United States' bases included some of the Aleutian Islands, off the tip of Alaska; Wake Island and tiny Midway Island in the Central Pacific; the Philippine Islands and Guam, in the Southwest Pacific, and others. The biggest and most important American naval base was on the Hawaiian Island of Oahu—the base called Pearl Harbor.

At ten minutes to eight o'clock on the morning of December 7, 1941, the sky over Pearl Harbor was bright, clear, and empty. In the harbor a large part of the U.S. Navy's Pacific Fleet lay peacefully at anchor—eight big battleships, eight cruisers, twenty-nine destroyers, and more than a score of various other ships. They were an imposing sight, advertising the might of one of the world's greatest sea powers.

Suddenly, clusters of dots appeared in the bright sky; dots that grew swiftly into low-flying airplanes rushing toward the island. In moments, the air was vibrating with the thunder of many motors as the formations of planes swept over Oahu. Startled eyes looked up from the ships and the shore and saw that the planes now fanning out over the harbor and island bore on their sides and wings the round, red ball that was the rising sun symbol of the empire of Japan. There was a sudden, startling *CR-RUMP* of an exploding bomb. Pearl Harbor was being attacked!

That surprise attack, which marked the beginning of 1,336 days of war between the United States and Japan in the Pacific Ocean, was a great success for the Japanese military forces. When the last of the planes went speeding back to their aircraft carriers lying far out at sea, the American fleet was lying under a shroud of smoke, badly crippled. Bombs had sunk three of the battleships, turned another one over, and seriously damaged the other four. Three cruisers and three destroyers were also damaged, more than 260 airplanes had been destroyed, and more than three thousand men of the Navy, Marine Corps, and Army were dead. Luckily for the Americans, the fleet's three aircraft carriers, together with a number of other ships, were safely out at sea during the attack, and so escaped damage, but the loss of the battleships in the harbor was a shattering blow that meant the

An aerial view of Pearl Harbor

United States would begin the war at a serious disadvantage. The U.S. Navy had long had plans for what to do in case war broke out in the Pacific, but now those plans would have to be changed. American strategy had called for large forces, that included many battleships, to seize certain Japanese bases and to go quickly to the aid of British naval forces in the southwest. But the loss of so many battleships at Pearl Harbor made this impossible. The American fleet could not go on the attack now; could not be risked on any long-range missions. The ships that were left would have to be kept back and used only in defense.

The Japanese, too, had long had plans for a war in the Pacific, and it was those plans they were now following. Their first goal had been to damage as badly as possible the U.S. Pacific Fleet, which was the only naval force in the Pacific strong enough to cause them any trouble (most of the powerful British fleet was in the Atlantic, engaged in the life-or-death struggle against Nazi Germany). The first part of the plan had been carried out with the attack on Pearl Harbor. Another objective was the quick capture of the rich oil fields in British Malaya and the Dutch (Netherlands) East Indies, for the Japanese Empire had no other way of getting the oil and gasoline it so desperately needed. At the same time, Japanese forces would seize many bases, to form a defensive ring around their conquests. They would then use these bases to smash any moves against them by the Allies—Americans, British, Australians and Dutch.

The Japanese moved swiftly to carry out their plans. Ten hours after Pearl Harbor was attacked, Japanese bombers winging from a base on the island of Formosa (present-day Taiwan) struck at the big, important U.S. Army Air Corps base of Clark Field, on the Philippine island of Luzon, and destroyed the majority of the American planes there. Almost at the same moment, Japanese forces invaded British Malaya and moved into the nation of Thailand, lying just next to the British colony of Burma. On December 10, with no American aircraft left to hinder them, Japanese ships began landing troops in the Philippines. On the same day, some 6,000 Japanese troops swarmed onto the American island base of Guam and quickly captured it from the tiny force of U.S. Marines and Guamanian police who tried to defend it. And on the same day still, Japanese bombers located the only two British battleships in the Pacific, which were hurrying to try to stop the landings on Malaya, and sank them. The Allies now had no battleships in the Pacific. The Japanese had eleven.

On December 11, the governments of Germany and Italy declared war on the United States. This was done because Germany and Italy, allies against Great Britain and Russia in the war going on in Europe and North Africa, had an alliance with Japan and were pledged to support it if it went to war. The German and Italian leaders were delighted to see Japan go to war against their enemy Great Britain, and were more than willing to go to war themselves against the United States, which had been doing all it could to help Great Britain and Russia, sending them supplies by sea.

So the United States, with its crippled Pacific Fleet, now found itself in two wars. And the war in the Pacific, which had begun so disastrously, continued that way. In the last three weeks of 1941 and the first few months of 1942, the Japanese army and navy continued to strike like a whirlwind at America and its friends in the Pacific. After a long, heroic struggle by the U.S. Marines defending it, the naval base of Wake Island was captured. The important British base of Hong Kong, on the coast of China, was captured. The Australian-controlled islands of New Britain were invaded, and the big, important port of Rabaul fell into Japanese hands, becoming Japan's main naval and air base in the Southwest Pacific. A powerful Japanese force moved into the Dutch East Indies (Indonesia), a mass of many thousands of big and little islands lying scattered between Australia and the southern tip of Asia. By the beginning of March, this entire area was captured, giving Japan control of vital oilfields, together with many bases from which to make attacks on Australia. Moving up out of Thailand, a Japanese army invaded Burma and pushed toward the border of India. In Malaya, British forces were pushed down into the island stronghold of Singapore, at the southern tip. On February 8, the Japanese stormed into Singapore and within a week it had surrendered. Seventy thousand British soldiers became prisoners of war. And in the Philippines, the American forces were being pushed back . . . back . . .

The Japanese did not go *entirely* unpunished. In January the American aircraft carrier *Yorktown*, which had been in the Atlantic, came around through the Panama Canal and joined the Pacific Fleet. With the four carriers and the undamaged cruisers and destroyers available, Admiral Chester W. Nimitz, who had been appointed commander in chief of the U.S. Pacific Fleet, put together small fleets known as task forces, and sent them out to cautiously do what damage they could. In late February, a task force headed by the carrier *Enterprise*, commanded by Vice Admiral William F. Halsey, launched a bombing attack on the Japanese troops that had taken over Wake Island. On March 10, a task force containing the carriers *Lexington* and *Yorktown* bombed Japanese bases in New Guinea, sinking and damaging a number of small ships.

But these were tiny "nuisance" raids that were hardly even heard of by the American people. On the other hand, the sweeping victories of the Japanese had made Americans grim and disheartened. It seemed as if America's Pacific enemy was unbeatable! On the West Coast, many people feared that a Japanese invasion might be made at any moment!

However, the Japanese war leaders, the generals and admirals who made the plans for how the war would be fought, had no thought at all of ever trying to invade and conquer the United States. The basis of their plans had been to knock out the U.S. fleet at Pearl Harbor and then to quickly capture so much territory that the United States would realize it would take a tremendous effort to get it all back, and faced with fighting another war in Europe (which many American politicians regarded as far more important than the one in the Pacific), would finally just drop out of the Pacific war in a year or so, letting the Japanese keep all their conquests. Most of the Japanese leaders felt that if the war dragged on for much more than two years, their chances of *losing* it would grow, because the vast industrial power of the United States could turn out far more ships, planes, tanks, and weapons over a long period of time than Japanese industry could. Japan's only hope for keeping all its conquests—many of which were vital to its national economy—was to make the United States drop out of the war in the Pacific as quickly as possible. As far as the war in Europe, and the fate of their German and Italian "allies" were concerned, the Japanese really didn't care.

But despite all their successes in the first few months of the war, the Japanese had not quite accomplished everything they needed to accomplish, for they hadn't damaged the American fleet as badly as they had hoped to. It was still able to cause them some trouble, as it had shown with those "nuisance" raids, and as long as it still existed it gave the American people confidence. But if most of what remained of it could be wiped out, so that the United States would have virtually no defense against attacks on Hawaii or even on the American West Coast, most Japanese leaders believed that would be enough to make the Americans want to quit and try to make peace. Therefore, it seemed obvious that the remaining American fleet had to be dealt a deathblow.

The commander in chief of the Japanese fleet, Admiral Isoroku Yamamoto, had a plan to bring that about. His plan was simply to trick the remaining American warships into going to a place where they could be attacked and destroyed by a much larger number of Japanese ships lying in wait for them. Yamamoto felt he could make the Americans come where he wanted them by capturing something they would absolutely *have* to try to get back—one of their most important bases, Midway Island.

Midway is what is called an "atoll"—a ring-shaped island

formed of stony coral, with a sort of small lake of sea water (called a "lagoon") in the middle of it. Midway Atoll is a partial ring of coral reef about six miles across, with a pair of tiny islands of dazzling white coral sand forming part of the ring. It lies almost exactly midway between Japan and the American West Coast, and the United States had turned it into a valuable naval base in the years before the war began. Huge stores of fuel and supplies were kept on Midway's islands, Sand Island and Eastern Island, and U.S. Navy ships, especially submarines, could sail in and drop anchor in the lagoon, take on fuel and supplies, and sail out again to attack Japanese warships. From airfields on the islands, planes flew out hundreds of miles over the ocean each day to spy out Japanese ship movements. Thus, in American hands, Midway was a threat to Japan, but in Japanese hands it would be a worse threat to the United States, for it could become a base from which attacks on Hawaii and even on the American West Coast could easily be made. If Midway were taken by the Japanese, Admiral Yamamoto felt sure the Americans would have no choice but to send what was left of their fleet to try to recapture it.

Admiral Yamamoto's plan called for a huge, powerful naval force to head secretly for Midway while a smaller force sailed northward and attacked American bases in the Aleutian Islands, to draw the attention of the American naval commanders there. Then, part of the fleet that sailed to Midway would launch a surprise air attack on the base, to "soften it up," and another part of the fleet would quickly land troops to wipe out the defenders and take over. The main portion of the Japanese force would lie back in hiding until the American ships came rushing to Midway's aid, and then the Japanese would close in and destroy the badly outnumbered Americans.

But not all the other Japanese military leaders would agree to Yamamoto's plan. Admiral Osami Nagano, the chief of the navy's general staff, whose main job it was to work out details of battle plans, wanted to make an invasion of Austra-

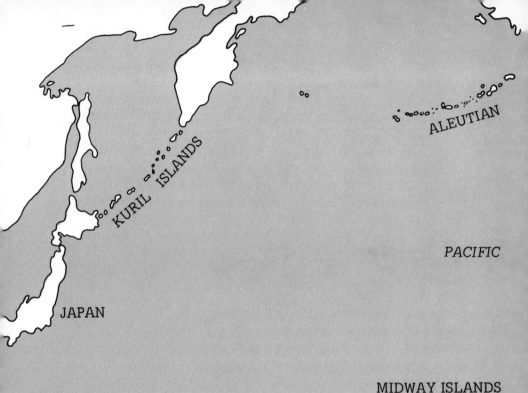

ALEUTIAN

PACIFIC

KURIL ISLANDS

JAPAN

MIDWAY ISLANDS

WAKE

MARIANA
ISLANDS

SAIPAN

GUAM

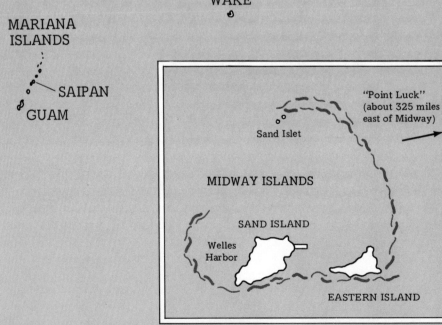

Sand Islet

"Point Luck"
(about 325 miles
east of Midway)

MIDWAY ISLANDS

SAND ISLAND

Welles
Harbor

EASTERN ISLAND

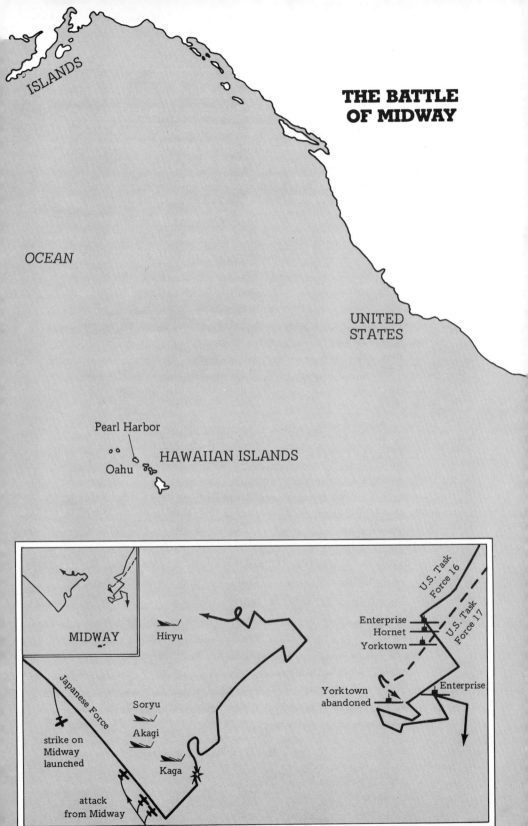

THE BATTLE
OF MIDWAY

ISLANDS

OCEAN

UNITED
STATES

Pearl Harbor

Oahu   HAWAIIAN ISLANDS

MIDWAY

Hiryu

Japanese Force

strike on
Midway
launched

Soryu

Akagi

Kaga

attack
from Midway

U.S. Task
Force 16

Enterprise
Hornet
Yorktown

U.S. Task
Force 17

Yorktown
abandoned

Enterprise

lia rather than Midway, fearing that Midway might not be important enough to bring the American ships into a trap. However, the army generals objected to Nagano's idea, pointing out that they simply didn't have enough troops for such a gigantic operation. Nagano then offered a plan to invade Fiji, the huge island just north of Australia, and to capture Samoa, a cluster of sixteen islands in the South Pacific less than 5,000 miles (8,000 km) from the American West Coast, where the United States had another important naval base. But Yamamoto refused to consider this and continued to insist on his own plan. For a time, the Japanese high command could not reach agreement.

Then, something happened that shocked the Japanese and thrilled the American people and their allies. On April 18, 1942, the Japanese capital, Tokyo, and nearby cities of Nagoya, Osaka, and Kobe, were bombed by sixteen U.S. Army B-25 bombers. The aircraft came roaring over Japan in broad daylight, catching fighter plane defenders and antiaircraft guns by surprise. The planes unloaded bombs that started fires and damaged steel plants and ammunition factories, and then sped away over Japan. Some of them later landed safely in China, an American ally; one came down in Russia, another ally; several crashed.

It seemed impossible. These bombers had only what was called a 600-mile (960-km) range, meaning they could carry only enough fuel to travel 600 miles from where they took off, and then turn and fly the 600 miles back—or, a total of 1,200 miles (1,920 km) one-way. Thus, the B-25s must have taken off from somewhere that was within at least 1,200 miles of Japan—except that the United States didn't have any bases

A B-25 bomber takes off from the deck of the Hornet *for the dramatic raid on Tokyo.*

that close! When President Roosevelt announced the bombing attack to the American people, he said only that the bombers had flown from "Shangri-la." But this meant nothing, for "Shangri-la" was simply the made-up name of a mysterious hidden city in a book of fiction by an English writer. There was no such place.

Actually, the bombers had taken off from the deck of the U.S. aircraft carrier *Hornet*, which had sailed to within 700 miles (1,120 km) of Japan. No one even considered that such huge planes, which generally needed a long strip of land from which to take off, could *possibly* have used the deck of a carrier. But the bomber crews, under the command of Lieutenant Colonel James H. "Jimmy" Doolittle, had trained until they were able to get off an aircraft carrier flight deck safely.

The bombings didn't do a great deal of damage, and were really just another nuisance raid. But they greatly cheered up the American people, who hadn't had much to be cheerful about up to now, and they frightened and enraged the Japanese, for whom the bombing of their homeland was a dreadful insult and humiliation. The Japanese leaders were so furious that when a few of the American bomber crewmen were captured, instead of having them all made prisoners of war, according to international law, the men were put on trial as war criminals, and several of them were executed by beheading.

The American bombing raid brought the Japanese high command to agreement. It seemed to the generals and admirals that there was only one possible place from which the bombers could have taken off, and that was Midway, which was just 2,300 miles (3,680 km) from Tokyo. Perhaps the bombers had carried extra fuel somehow, to enable them to make such a long flight, but at any rate, the danger of any more such raids had to be eliminated. Midway had to be captured! There was agreement that Admiral Yamamoto's plan should be carried out.

And now there took place another event that strengthened the belief of the Japanese leaders that the American fleet had to be wiped out. On the third of May a Japanese force moved into the Solomon Islands, a chain of islands near the northwestern part of Australia, and landed troops on the islands of Tulagi and Florida Island. Then, the force of warships, which included two aircraft carriers and troop transports, moved out of the Solomons into a stretch of water known as the Coral Sea, on the way to make an invasion of Port Moresby, an extremely important Allied base on the big island of Papua New Guinea, very close to Australia. But in the Coral Sea the Japanese met one of Admiral Nimitz's troublesome task forces, and a major battle took place—the Battle of the Coral Sea. While the Americans lost *Lexington,* one of their only four carriers in the Pacific, plus an oil tanker and a destroyer, the Japanese lost only a light aircraft carrier and a few other ships. But the Japanese had to turn back, and give up the Port Moresby invasion. Clearly, the American warships that remained were a threat that had to be eliminated.

So, on May 5, Admiral Yamamoto's plan was accepted by all the other war leaders, and the buildup of the attack force began. Huge amounts of food, fuel, and other supplies were collected at the bases from which various parts of the force would sail. The troops that were to land on the two little islands at Midway and the pilots who would make the "softening-up" air raid began to train in secret. The ships that were to take part were supplied and fueled, while their crews were brought up to full strength. The admirals who would command the various parts of the force held frequent secret meetings to check and recheck their plans.

The different parts of the attack force sailed from Japan and the islands of Guam and Saipan between May 26 and May 28. Altogether they formed the biggest war fleet ever seen in the Pacific Ocean. There were four of Japan's biggest, fastest aircraft carriers, two light carriers, two seaplane carriers, seven battleships, thirteen cruisers, some forty destroyers, about sixteen submarines, and a large number of supply and troop transport ships. As the ships headed out to sea they rocked with the noise of cheering and the wild singing of patriotic songs. The Japanese sailors felt they were on the way to a tremendous victory that would literally knock their enemy out of the war.

CHAPTER

THE
ATTACK ON
MIDWAY

The success of Admiral Yamamoto's plan depended mainly on secrecy and surprise. But unfortunately for the Japanese, they couldn't keep their preparations secret, and thus they were unable to take the Americans by surprise.

The Japanese did not know that the secret code they used in sending radio messages to ships, planes, and troop commanders was *not* secret; the Americans had pretty well figured it out. But the Japanese continued to use it, with the result that many supposedly secret messages dealing with the buildup of the Midway attack force were intercepted by American ship and shore radios and decoded by American naval intelligence officers, whose job it was to find out what the enemy was going to do. Reports were also coming in from American submarines patrolling near the places where the Japanese ships were assembling, and from other sources. Thus, by the middle of May, Admiral Nimitz not only knew what the Japanese were planning, but also had a good idea of how many and what kinds of ships they would use. He even had a fair idea of when the attack would be made. Admiral Yamamoto had been right that the Americans wouldn't let Midway fall into Japanese hands without risking everything they had to prevent it, and Admiral Nimitz began calling every available U.S. warship into Pearl Harbor to form a fleet to defend the vital base.

The fleet that was finally put together seemed woefully small. To stand up to the huge attack force that he knew the Japanese were sending, Nimitz had only three aircraft carriers, eight cruisers, seventeen destroyers, and twenty-five submarines, together with a couple of fuel tankers. (Actually, Nimitz did have a few more ships available, but he formed them into a tiny fleet to be sent to the Aleutians, just in case the Japanese "pretend" attack there turned out to be the main attack after all, which was what some American admirals feared.) The U.S. fleet would be both outnumbered and outgunned, but it *would* have two advantages—the Japanese wouldn't be expecting to run into it, and it would have a lot of help from the planes based on Midway, which would be like a huge, unsinkable aircraft carrier. At any rate, outnumbered and outgunned or not, the little fleet was the best the U.S. Navy could do; it would have to do its best.

Admiral Nimitz divided the Midway fleet into two parts that were given the names "Task Force 16" and "Task Force 17." Task Force 16 consisted of the aircraft carriers *Hornet* and *Enterprise,* plus six cruisers, eleven destroyers, and two tankers. It was to be commanded by Rear Admiral Raymond A. Spruance, who was sometimes known as "the human machine," because he had a mind like a computer and never seemed to get excited. Task Force 17 consisted of the carrier *Yorktown,* with two cruisers and six destroyers, and would be commanded by Rear Admiral Frank Jack Fletcher, who had been the commander at the Battle of the Coral Sea. Fletcher would actually be the man in charge of both task forces. The submarines, under the command of Rear Admiral Robert English, would be placed in a long patrol line where they could quickly report any sightings of the enemy force and do whatever damage possible with their torpedoes.

Once the battle fleet was put together, Admiral Nimitz turned his attention to making Midway into a fortress. The base was already pretty well equipped to defend itself; with six big naval guns, a dozen antiaircraft guns, almost a hundred machine guns, a squadron of Marine fighter planes and a squadron of scout bombers, and over 700 marines. But from about the twentieth of May to the beginning of June, more weapons, planes, and men were poured in to add to Midway's defenses—sixteen Marine dive bombers, twenty-two army bombers, and another half-dozen fighter planes; more antiaircraft guns, more marines, and even five light tanks. Bombproof shelters were constructed, underwater mines were scattered all around the reef, and wild tangles of spiky barbed wire were strung on the reef and the island beaches.

On May 28, Task Force 16 quietly left Pearl Harbor, and Task Force 17 departed two days later, taking a slightly different course. On June 2 the two forces came together again at a spot in the ocean that had been designated "Point Luck," about 325 miles (520 km) northeast of Midway. There, they waited.

Every day since May 30, twenty-two big U.S. Navy PBY flying boats, known as "Catalinas," had been flying patrols from Midway, searching the sea as far out as 700 miles (1,120 km) in all directions from the base, watching for enemy ships. A little before nine o'clock on the morning of June 3, Ensign Jack Reid, at the controls of a Catalina just about 700 miles southwest of Midway, leaned forward and peered through his binoculars at a distant point on the vast sheet of gray-green water spread out beyond his plane's nose. "Do you see what I see?" he asked his co-pilot. They both agreed on what they saw—eleven ships heading toward Midway at top speed. Ensign Reid sent a message to Midway that the Japanese were beginning to arrive.

The commanders on Midway believed that the ships coming toward them were part of the Japanese main fleet, because Reid said he thought he saw battleships and cruisers among them. But Admiral Fletcher—who of course was being notified of everything that was happening—wasn't so sure. From what he had learned from naval intelligence reports on the Japanese plan, it seemed to him that the main Japanese force would not be coming straight from the southwest, as these ships were, but from the northwest. Fletcher thought about it for a while, then made a very important decision. He had the two task forces turn and sail toward where he felt the Japanese fleet would be coming from, the northwest.

Admiral Fletcher was absolutely right. The Japanese ships that had been sighted were not part of the main fleet; they were just some of the transports bringing the Japanese marines and soldiers who were supposed to land on Midway and capture it. The advance portion of Admiral Yamamoto's main fleet *was* approaching Midway from the northwest and was now only a few hundred miles distant. Thanks to Fletcher's decision, the American ships were heading straight for it.

The advance portion of the Japanese main fleet was made up of two battleships, two cruisers, twelve destroyers, some tankers—and the four big aircraft carriers. The carriers were actually the "backbone" of this force, and the other ships were there mainly just to protect them. The planes on the carriers were to be launched in a tremendous bombing attack on Midway to knock out the defenses so the troops coming from the southwest, on the transports, could land and take over the base with little or no trouble. Like the American carriers, the Japanese ships held three different kinds of planes—dive bombers, which swooped down on a target from a great height and dropped a single, large bomb; torpedo planes, which came in low and straight at a target and launched a torpedo; and heavily armed fighter planes, whose job it was to protect the bombers and torpedo planes by shooting down any enemy aircraft that tried to attack them. For an attack on a land target such as Midway, both the dive bombers and torpedo planes would carry bombs, for torpedoes would not, of course, work on land. The four carriers— *Akagi* (Red Castle), *Kaga* (Increased Joy), *Soryu* (Green Dragon), and *Hiryu* (Flying Dragon)—bore a total of 272 planes, which was about forty more than the three American carriers could put into the sky.

As the Japanese advance force sped toward Midway in the hours of early morning darkness on June 4, its commanding officer, Vice Admiral Chuichi Nagumo, who had commanded the attack on Pearl Harbor, was faintly worried. There were low, heavy rain clouds hanging thickly over this part of the ocean, and if they were still there by the time the planes were due to be launched, at about sunrise, it would make the launching and the entire attack far more difficult. But as the hours wore on the clouds began to rise and visibility became somewhat better. By four o'clock in the morning, the planes that would make the attack on Midway were warming up on the carrier flight decks and it looked as if conditions would be good enough. At four-thirty Admiral Nagumo gave the order to launch the attack.

As each plane roared along the deck and lifted into the lightening sky, the carrier crews flung up their arms and raised a great shout of "Banzai," or "Forever," meaning that the glory of the empire of Japan would last forever. By sunup, a little before five o'clock, 108 Japanese warplanes were droning toward Midway.

On Midway, between 4:15 and 4:30, eleven Catalinas had taken off, each heading for a different section of ocean on reconnaissance missions. They were flying high enough to be able to see a lot of ocean, but for those heading northwest the thick clouds blocked most of the view of the water. However, at about 5:30 the pilot of one of the Catalinas found an opening in the clouds and nosed down through it. Within minutes he and his crew spotted the Japanese carriers and saw the formations of planes winging off toward Midway. A radio message went flashing back to the atoll and to the American fleet—"Enemy carriers. Many planes heading Midway." And a few minutes later another Catalina also located the Japanese and radioed vital information—"Two carriers and battleships, bearing 320 degrees, distance 180, course 135, speed 25."

Admiral Fletcher now knew exactly where his enemy was. He had sent a number of *Yorktown*'s planes out on patrol that morning and now had to wait for them to return before he could take *Yorktown* after the Japanese ships, but he ordered Admiral Spruance to take Task Force 16 toward the Japanese position and launch an attack, promising to bring Task Force 17 to join in as soon as all his planes were back. Soon, Spruance's two carriers and other ships were closing toward Nagumo's force at top speed.

Meanwhile, on Midway, air raid sirens were howling, marines were rushing to their battle stations, and every plane that could fly was getting into the air. Two squadrons of Marine fighter planes were rising up to take on the incoming Japanese aircraft, while two flights of Marine bombers sped toward the enemy carriers, followed by half a dozen navy torpedo planes and four army B-26 high-level bombers.

Thirty miles (48 km) out from Midway the twelve planes of the first Marine fighter squadron that had taken off spotted the Japanese aircraft roaring toward them. The American planes climbed high, hoping to take their enemy by surprise, and swept down in screaming dives. Thirty-six Japanese fighters swarmed up to meet them. A twisting, turning dogfight began, with planes suddenly blown apart in midair, falling in flames into the ocean below, gliding down crippled to crash-land in the water. Not only did the Americans face three-to-one odds, but more than half of them were flying old-model planes that were no match at all for the swifter, more agile Japanese Zero fighters. The badly outnumbered and outclassed marines managed to knock out two Zeroes, but the squadron was practically wiped out.

Just outside the atoll the Japanese were met by the second Marine fighter squadron of thirteen planes. Most of these Americans were also flying old Brewster Buffaloes which were no match for the Zeroes, and the result of this fight was the same as the first. Of the total of twenty-five American fighter planes that left Midway to attack the incoming Japanese aircraft, seventeen were destroyed and seven badly damaged. Only a few managed to make it back to the atoll after the Japanese attack ended.

The Japanese bombers and torpedo planes roared in over Midway's two islands and were met by a hail of antiaircraft and machine-gun fire. The islands shuddered as dozens of 550-pound bombs struck with thunderous explosions. A cluster of fuel storage tanks erupted with a deafening *WHUMP*, sending a coiling cloud of greasy black smoke rushing into the sky. A bomb slammed into the powerhouse on Eastern Island; another burst inside a big seaplane hangar, setting it afire; others demolished the mess hall where the marines had their meals, and the dispensary where they received medical care.

But the sky was literally filled with streams of machine-gun bullets and speckled with the black puffs of bursting antiaircraft shells, and these were taking a toll of the raiders. A Japanese fighter had its wing sliced off by a spray of .50-caliber machine-gun bullets, and went cartwheeling into the sand. A bomber came spinning down out of the sky trailing a plume of black smoke. Another bomber disintegrated in midair. The full-throated roar of airplane engines, the stutter of scores of machine guns, and the shattering *kBLAM* of 3-inch antiaircraft guns mixed into an ear-splitting, mind-numbing din of violence.

After ten minutes of this terrible destruction on land and in the sky, the Japanese planes swung off and headed back out over the ocean. The atoll lay beneath an umbrella of smoke, and a dozen fires flickered among the shattered buildings. But thanks to the advance warning and days of preparation, the number of dead and injured was surprisingly small. The precious runways on which planes could land and take off were still in good shape, and there were plenty of guns left and plenty of men to use them. Midway was wounded, but it was far from crippled, and a long, long way from being dead!

This was quite clear to the commander of the Japanese aircraft as he led his planes back to their carriers. He had noted that the airfield runways were still in good enough condition to be used, and that the antiaircraft fire had been as vicious when his planes were leaving as it had been when they arrived. Obviously, the attack had not been a success. But Midway's defenses *had* to be knocked out before the Japanese troops tried to land or they would be slaughtered! The commander sent a radio message to Admiral Nagumo— "Second attack necessary!"

When Nagumo received that message it meant he had to make a serious decision. His fleet was in a good, safe situation, with dozens of Zero fighters circling protectively over it and with a total of ninety-three torpedo planes and dive bombers sitting on the decks of the carriers, armed and ready to be launched. But if another attack on Midway was needed, it should be made right away, and these planes and the fighters overhead would have to be sent to make it. This meant that with them gone, and the planes that had made the first attack not back yet, the four carriers would have no aircraft protection for several hours, and would be helpless if attacked by American planes from Midway—should any of them manage to get into the air and past his attacking force. So Nagumo had to decide—should he make a second attack on Midway, and risk danger to his carriers, or should he not attack and possibly risk having the whole invasion defeated because Midway's defenses were still in good shape?

While he was pondering this, sirens signaling an air raid alert began to wail on his ships. Some of the American planes from Midway that he had been concerned about had just arrived—six U.S. Navy Grumman Avenger torpedo planes and four U.S. Army B-26 bombers. But this tiny force had no chance at all. The warships that were surrounding Nagumo's carriers in a protective "box" formation opened up with every antiaircraft gun they had. They shot seven of the American planes right out of the sky and sent the other three limping off, badly damaged, to crash-land on Midway hours later.

The result of this pitiful attack was that Nagumo was able

to make up his mind about sending the rest of his planes to make a second assault on Midway. His ships had fought off the American planes so easily that the admiral now felt he had nothing to fear from any other planes that might come from the atoll. He ordered a second attack to be made.

However, Nagumo had ordered all the torpedo planes sitting on the carrier flight decks to be armed with torpedoes just in case any American ships should show up. So before those planes could be sent to Midway they would have to have their torpedoes replaced with bombs for use on land targets. Crews began hauling the planes onto the huge elevators, where they were carried down to the decks below to have the torpedoes removed and bombs installed. Thus, by about 7:30 that morning, a good half of Nagumo's planes were disarmed and down off the flight decks, and it would be a long time before they could be rearmed, made ready to fly, and brought back up.

And at that moment, Nagumo received another radio message. He really didn't think there were any American ships within a thousand miles (1,600 km) or so, but just in case, he had sent out seven scout planes just after sunrise, to look around. None of them had apparently seen anything. However, one of them had been a little late in taking off because of a mechanical problem, and it had just now reached the farthest point of its search area—and there it *had* seen something. Its message said, "Have seen what appears

The Japanese carrier Kaga sails in a complete circle to avoid American bombers during the Battle of Midway. The Kaga was one of four Japanese carriers lost in that battle.

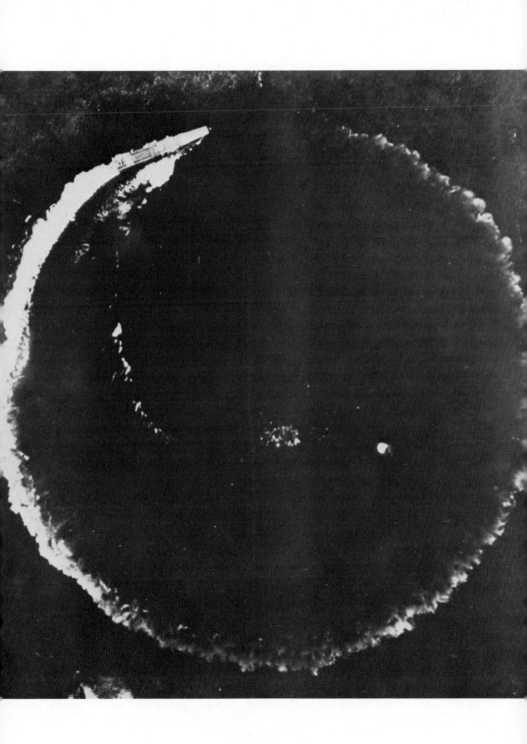

to be ten enemy ships in position bearing 10 degrees, distance 240 miles [384 km] from Midway."

Nagumo was thunderstruck! There *was* an American fleet nearby, and if it included an aircraft carrier, then his own carrier force was in terrible danger of being hit by a heavy air attack at a moment when more than half his planes were down on the hangar decks with their wings folded up and their torpedoes being removed!

Nagumo now seemed to become uncertain about what he should do. He ordered the carrier crews to stop removing the torpedoes and to stand by for an air attack against ships instead of against a land base. He sent a message to the scout plane that had sighted the Americans demanding to know what *kinds* of ships it had seen. Apparently, he felt that he had to find out whether or not any of those ships were carriers before he could decide exactly what to do.

Then, as Nagumo paced back and forth on the bridge of his flagship, *Akagi,* waiting for an answer to his message, something happened that made his problem even more complicated. The rest of the American planes from Midway arrived, and the Japanese fleet came under attack.

The Americans came in three groups, one after the other—first sixteen Marine dive bombers, then fifteen U.S. Army high-level B-26 bombers, then eleven Marine Vindicator bombers—a total of forty-two planes. They flew through swarms of the deadly Zero fighters and through hailstorms of machine-gun fire and antiaircraft bursts. Some were shot down before they could even drop their bombs; the others managed to unload their bombs and get away. But in what seemed to be an almost incredible flow of bad luck for the Americans and good luck for the Japanese, not one of the many bombs dropped hit anything. The attack was a total failure.

However, it was 8:30 by the time the last American plane was chased off. The attack had taken nearly a full hour, and during that time the Japanese had not, of course, been able to bring any planes up from the carrier hangar decks to the flight decks. So Admiral Nagumo was actually in a slightly worse predicament than he had been in before the attack began. For one thing, he had finally received the answer he had been awaiting from the scout plane and it had confirmed his worst fears—the pilot indicated that he thought he had, indeed, seen an aircraft carrier among the American ships. But even though Nagumo now knew without question that there was at least one American carrier within striking distance, there was still nothing he could do. He still couldn't start bringing planes up onto the carrier decks, because the planes from his Midway attack force were just now beginning to return, and the decks had to be kept clear so they could land. The Japanese carriers were going to continue to be sitting ducks for some time.

Desperate with anxiety, Nagumo waited as plane after plane, each nearly out of fuel, came gliding onto its carrier's deck. By 8:45, he was growing even more anxious, for he was now getting messages from some of the other scout planes, reporting large flights of aircraft heading toward his ships, and he knew what that meant—the American carrier had launched an attack!

At seventeen minutes past nine, with most of his planes now safely back and covering the decks of their carriers, Nagumo ordered his fleet to change course to a right angle from its original direction. He intended to hide out under some heavy clouds that would conceal his force from the American aircraft while he got all his planes refueled and properly armed—then he would launch an all-out attack that would cripple the little American fleet and leave it helpless, to be destroyed by the big guns of the battleships of the Japanese main force. Even though the Americans had apparently somehow found out about the Midway invasion, Admiral Yamamoto's plan would still work to crush them.

CHAPTER III

THE AMERICAN COUNTERBLOW

At seven o'clock, just about the same moment when Admiral Nagumo was trying to decide whether to make a second attack on Midway, the commander of American Task Force 16, Admiral Spruance, was also pondering a difficult decision. Spruance knew the Japanese planes were now returning from the attack on Midway, and if he launched every plane he could right *now*, they had a good chance of reaching the Japanese fleet just as the Japanese planes were landing on their carriers, which meant the carriers would be helpless. On the other hand, if the American task force had been spotted by Japanese scout planes, a Japanese air attack might be headed toward it this very moment, and with all their planes gone it was the American carriers that would be defenseless.

But Spruance quickly made up his mind to take a daring chance—he ordered every plane that could fly to take off and go after the Japanese fleet. About half an hour later, Task Force 17 joined Spruance's force, and Admiral Fletcher launched about half of *Yorktown*'s planes. Thus, at 9:17, when Admiral Nagumo ordered his fleet to change course, 151 American planes were streaking toward the part of the ocean where the last Catalina report had said Nagumo's ships could be found.

But Nagumo's order to change course had been a smart move that caused the American pilots a good deal of trouble. For, as each American squadron reached the place where the Japanese fleet was supposed to be it found nothing there. Each squadron commander had to decide immediately which way to go to search for the enemy.

The planes from *Hornet* came toward the position all together; thirty-five dive bombers and nine fighters up high, and fifteen torpedo planes down low. When the officer leading the bombers and fighters realized the Japanese fleet wasn't where it was supposed to be, he decided it must have moved closer to Midway, so he led his planes in that direction. Of course, they never found the Japanese ships.

The commander of the squadron of low-flying torpedo planes couldn't see the fighters and bombers turn toward Midway because they were hidden from him by clouds. So when he decided to take his squadron northward—the right direction—his fifteen planes were all by themselves, with no fighters to protect them and no dive bombers to help them with an attack.

Shortly, the torpedo squadron sighted smoke from the stacks of Japanese ships in the distance and turned toward it. They were still miles from the enemy fleet when Zeroes began to pounce on them from all sides. Grimly, each pilot tried to twist and weave his way through danger, moving steadily toward the Japanese ships, while each rear gunner tried desperately to fight off the two or three Zeroes clinging to his craft's tail with their guns chattering. Antiaircraft bursts began to hurl chunks of shrapnel into the torpedo planes, and machine-gun tracer bullets, leaving long thin trails of white smoke to show their path, were reaching toward the Americans from all sides. Planes began dropping out of the formation, riddled with bullets, shattered by antiaircraft fire, burning. All fifteen planes of *Hornet's* Torpedo Squadron 8 were shot down and none of the few torpedoes they managed to launch scored a hit.

A squadron of Douglas "Devastator"
torpedo bombers unfold their hinged wings,
ready for takeoff from the U.S.S. Enterprise
during the Battle of Midway.

Only moments after the last of *Hornet's* torpedo planes went down, Torpedo Squadron 6, from *Enterprise*, found the Japanese ships and came buzzing in low over the water to make their attack. But these planes, too, had become separated from their fighters and had no protection from the Zeroes. Ten of the fourteen planes were destroyed before they could even launch torpedoes. The other four managed to launch and then dodge away from the pursuing Zeroes, but none of their torpedoes hit anything.

By now it was ten o'clock, and still another squadron of American torpedo planes had appeared. This was *Yorktown's* Torpedo Squadron 3. It was accompanied by six Wildcat fighter planes, but they were, of course, vastly outnumbered by all the Zeroes, and while a few Zeroes dealt with them, the rest swarmed over the torpedo planes. Although seven of the Americans went down in flames, five managed to launch before three of them were shot down. Once again, however, there were no torpedo hits.

The Japanese sailors on the carriers and other ships were jubilant! All morning long they had been fighting off air attacks, first from the Midway planes and now from carriers, and they hadn't even been scratched. It seemed like incredible good luck and an incredible victory over the attacking Americans.

But the good luck was suddenly about to turn very bad. By sheer chance, the seemingly useless torpedo plane attacks had made two things happen. One—during the attacks the Japanese had not been able to clear the carrier decks of aircraft and the decks were crowded with planes, just as Admiral Spruance had hoped. And, two—because all the attacks had been launched by torpedo planes flying nearly at sea level, all the Japanese fighter planes had come down low to attack the attackers. There were now *no* Zeroes high overhead. And high overhead, two groups of American Douglas Dauntless dive bombers were racing in toward the Japanese from two directions.

One group consisted of two squadrons from *Enterprise*,

which now split up, each squadron heading for a separate Japanese carrier. In moments, thirty-seven dive bombers were screaming down on their targets. There were no enemy fighters nearby to stop them, and hardly any antiaircraft fire, for most of the Japanese ships had not yet even become aware of the danger dropping upon them. The first three planes that dove at the carrier *Kaga* missed with their bombs. Then, a 1,000-pound bomb went off on *Kaga*'s deck with a searing flash and the impact of a giant fist. The superstructure, the multistoried, metal-walled housing that sits like a castle at the edge of a carrier's flight deck, became a twisted pile of bent steel plate and broken glass, filled with dead and dying men.

Moments later a second bomb erupted among the planes on the flight deck, hurling them in all directions and ripping a huge hole in the deck. Gasoline, pouring out of the gashed and split tanks of aircraft, caught fire, and a dozen flaming streams went zigzagging across the deck and dripped down through the jagged bomb crater onto the hangar deck below, starting fires there. Two more bombs shattered *Kaga*'s top deck and turned it into a raging sea of flames. The carrier was finished!

The carrier being attacked by the sixteen planes of the other squadron was *Akagi*, the flagship of the fleet, upon which Admiral Nagumo had his headquarters. Forty planes sat on its flight deck. They were fueled and armed and ready to be launched for the attack that Nagumo had planned to make against the American fleet, and everyone aboard the ship was watching them make ready to take off. But suddenly, *Akagi*'s crew became aware of another sound rising over the warmup rumble of their planes' engines—the shrill, screaming roar of diving aircraft. Heads jerked upward and eyes widened in shock at the sight of the U.S. Navy Helldivers streaking down at them.

The first bomb dropped was a near miss that showered *Akagi*'s deck with water. The second struck directly in the center of the flight deck just behind the elevator on which planes were carried down to or brought up from the hangar deck. Tearing through the flight deck, the bomb burst on the hangar deck, where a quantity of torpedoes had been stored, causing them to explode instantly. The double blast buckled the flight deck overhead, shattered the elevator, and set the hangar deck aflame. Moments later a second bomb exploded at the rear of the flight deck, hurling planes and men into the sea and starting a raging fire there. *Akagi*, too, was finished! The stunned and shaken Admiral Nagumo and some of his officers managed to make their way onto a destroyer that came alongside the burning carrier.

The other group of dive bombers that had managed to locate the Japanese fleet was the squadron from *Yorktown*, and this squadron made its attack on the carrier nearest to it, which happened to be *Soryu*. The American planes came screaming down at the carrier in three waves. A 1,000-pound bomb broke through *Soryu*'s flight deck and exploded on the hangar deck with a force that crumpled the carrier's forward elevator and slammed it against the ship's superstructure. A second bomb and then a third exploded on the flight deck and the whole ship burst into flames. Men with scorched uniforms and blackened skins began leaping into the sea. Within twenty minutes, *Soryu*'s captain ordered the entire crew to abandon ship.

The three bombing attacks had taken only two minutes, but during those 120 seconds the entire course of the Battle of Midway had changed. Admiral Nagumo's planned huge attack on the American fleet had been snuffed out before it could even get started, and he had lost three quarters of his carriers and three quarters of his planes. After completing their attack, the American dive bombers started heading back toward their carriers. Some were shot down before they could get away, some ran out of fuel and had to ditch in the ocean before they could reach their carrier. But of the fifty-four planes that had made the attack, thirty-eight got back to let Admirals Fletcher and Spruance know that the Japanese carrier force had been dealt a mortal blow.

However, the battle was far from over. The carrier *Hiryu* had not been seen by any of the American dive bombers because it was a considerable distance away from the other three carriers, and it had a full load of planes that were armed, fueled, and ready to launch. When Admiral Nagumo left the shattered *Akagi*, command of the Japanese carrier force temporarily went to the man who was in command of the cruisers and destroyers, Rear Admiral Hiroaki Abe, and Abe was determined to strike back at the Americans. He ordered *Hiryu*'s planes to be launched in an attack.

By eleven o'clock, eighteen of *Hiryu*'s dive bombers and six of its fighters were in the air. There were still a few American planes in sight, far in the distance, and the Japanese flight commander simply followed them, knowing they would lead him straight to their carrier. The American planes were from *Yorktown*, so it was *Yorktown* that would become the target of the Japanese attack.

Of course, both Admirals Fletcher and Spruance knew there was still a Japanese carrier left, and were expecting an attack from it. Both of them had forces of Wildcat fighters patrolling over their carriers. It was a little before noon when *Yorktown*'s patrol planes spotted the wave of enemy aircraft coming toward the ship. The twelve Wildcats scrambled to intercept the Japanese and shot down ten of the dive bombers. The cruisers and destroyers protecting *Yorktown* opened up with antiaircraft fire on the eight bombers that managed to get through the Wildcats, but even as one bomber was hit and blown apart, it dropped a bomb that burst on *Yorktown*'s flight deck, blowing open a hole and starting a fire on the hangar deck below. A few moments later, a bomb

Attacks by these Douglas
SBD Dauntless dive bombers
turned the Battle of Midway to
the United States' advantage.

exploded inside one of *Yorktown*'s smokestacks, sending a shower of burning soot throughout the ship and disabling several of the boilers that provided the carrier's power. Then a third bomb exploded below decks, starting more fires.

The other bombs dropped were misses. The eight surviving Japanese planes sped off, leaving *Yorktown* wounded but not really in bad shape. The fires were quickly put out, but the damage to the boilers caused the ship to lose speed gradually and then come to a full stop—which was noticed by the Japanese pilots. And because fire had damaged the communications system, Admiral Fletcher could no longer use *Yorktown* as his flagship, and had to move onto a cruiser.

However, by two o'clock that afternoon, *Yorktown*'s engines were working again and the carrier was once more able to move. And it could still put planes in the air—fighters were sitting on the main deck, being made ready for takeoff.

But the Japanese weren't through with *Yorktown*. The surviving Japanese pilots had notified their commander that the American carrier had been damaged and was in trouble. A second wave of planes—ten Nakajima torpedo planes and six Zeroes—was coming to try to finish the job.

They arrived about 2:30. Eight Wildcats sped to meet them and the American ships opened up with antiaircraft fire. But four of the Japanese planes managed to get through the fighters and antiaircraft barrage and launch their torpedoes. Two of the torpedoes slammed into the carrier's side and exploded with a sound like thunder. The explosions jammed the ship's rudder, knocked out all electrical power, and blew a hole in the hull that began to let in water. *Yorktown* started to lean over on its side. By three o'clock, the captain gave the order to abandon ship.

Even as the sailors were leaving the stricken *Yorktown*, the decks of *Hornet* and *Enterprise* were bustling with activity. Scout planes had located the last Japanese carrier and Admiral Spruance was now about to launch the heaviest possible attack against it, for as long as it was active and able to

The U.S. aircraft carrier Yorktown under attack at Midway. The column of black smoke to the left of the carrier is from a burning Japanese plane, and the puffs of smoke in the air, from antiaircraft fire.

launch planes, the two remaining American carriers were in serious danger. If *Hornet* and *Enterprise* were to get knocked out along with *Yorktown*, the Americans would lose the battle, lose Midway, and possibly lose the war. So at 3:30, twenty-four dive bombers from *Enterprise* and sixteen from *Hornet* rose from their flight decks to attack *Hiryu* and destroy it. At exactly five o'clock the *Enterprise* dive bombers reached *Hiryu*'s position.

Aboard *Hiryu* at that moment, planes were being refueled and rearmed for another attack, while the crew was being given the first meal it had been able to have since dawn. Patrol planes were circling over the carrier, but they apparently did not see the approaching American aircraft, which were coming from the west with the afternoon sun directly behind them, making them almost impossible to spot. The first anyone aboard *Hiryu* knew of the attack was when they became aware of that terrifying sound of screaming engines that meant diving airplanes. Someone yelled, "Helldivers!" Then the first bomb struck.

It tore the forward elevator loose and hurled it into the superstructure, also blasting a huge hole in the flight deck. Three more bombs burst, and the airplanes being made ready for launching were scattered in all directions, their bombs and torpedoes exploding and gasoline from their shattered tanks bursting into flame. The fires spread with incredible speed and were quickly out of control. When the dive bombers from *Hornet* arrived, they found *Hiryu* burning fiercely and shattered beyond any further use.

At ten minutes before ten o'clock that morning, Admiral Yamamoto, then hundreds of miles away with the main Japanese fleet, had received a message telling him of the loss of the three carriers, *Akagi, Kaga,* and *Soryu.* Now at five minutes to six o'clock in the evening he received another message from Admiral Nagumo. It said, "Bombs hit *Hiryu*, causing fires." Yamamoto read between the lines and understood that *Hiryu* was seriously damaged. It was obvious that his advance force no longer had any aircraft carriers.

However, Yamamoto believed he still had a chance to turn this stunning defeat into a victory after all. He sent messages to Nagumo, to the admiral in command of the troopships coming from the southwest, to all his submarines, and to the Japanese ships that had gone to the Aleutian Islands, giving orders to surround the American force with many ships and pound it to death with gunfire during the night.

But Admiral Spruance, now temporarily in command of the two U.S. task forces, knew very well that the Japanese would be looking for the American ships during the night, and he had no intention of letting his fleet be found or of fighting an old-fashioned "gunbattle" in darkness, with an enemy force that heavily outnumbered and outgunned him. As soon as all of the *Hornet* and *Enterprise* dive bombers had returned, he ordered all ships to pull back until they would be out of reach of the Japanese ships, but still in range to launch an air attack in the morning.

So as the Japanese ships crept through the darkness that night, searching for the American fleet, they found nothing. By 2:30 in the morning, June 5, Admiral Yamamoto realized that his whole great plan to destroy the U.S. Pacific Fleet had failed. He obviously wasn't going to be able to find the Americans during the night, but if he kept his ships where they were, the Americans would surely find *them* in the morning, with air attacks. Once again Yamamoto sent out many messages, calling ships together, turning ships around, pulling the entire Japanese fleet back . . . retreating. At five minutes before three o'clock a last, single message went out to all the Japanese ships: "Occupation of Midway is cancelled."

This was a dreadful blow for all the men of the Japanese fleet, for it meant they had been defeated. And this was the first defeat the modern Japanese navy had suffered since it had been formed. Admiral Yamamoto sat alone on the bridge of the Battleship *Yamoto*, sipping from a bowl of rice soup and staring bitterly into the darkness.

This Japanese cruiser Mikuma *sank on June 5
after marine planes from Midway attacked.*

Things were still not quite over for either the Japanese or Americans. During the next two days, American search planes sank one Japanese cruiser and badly damaged another, while a Japanese submarine torpedoed and finally sank the still-floating *Yorktown*, as well as an American destroyer. With that, the Battle of Midway officially came to an end.

It was a clear-cut victory for the United States. Four major Japanese aircraft carriers and one cruiser had been sunk, as against one American carrier and a destroyer. The American fleet was still in good fighting shape and Midway was still in American hands. When news of the battle's outcome was released in the United States, with newspaper headlines such as "Japanese Smashed at Midway," there was a tremendous uplifting of spirits. This was badly needed, for until then, of course, things had not been going well, either in the Pacific or in Europe.

In any war, a great many of the battles that are fought really do not make much of a difference, but the Battle of Midway was what historians call a "decisive battle"—an action whose outcome actually affects history. If the Japanese had won at Midway, the United States might well have made peace, as the Japanese hoped, and left Japan in control of the Pacific, which would have made the world a rather different place today. But the American victory meant that the war would continue, and this, as many of Japan's admirals and generals realized only too well, meant that Japan was going to lose: the longer America stayed in the war, the more war matériel its enormous industrial power could turn out. For Japan, a long war would be—and was—a strain its industry could not meet. The loss of the four carriers at Midway was a loss the Japanese shipbuilders were never able to make up, whereas the U.S. shipbuilding industry put nine new carriers out to sea before the war's end.

The Japanese had also lost 322 planes and hundreds of their best, most experienced pilots, and these, too, could not be replaced. Those pilots were men who could have taught their skills to younger Japanese airmen, and without them, there simply weren't enough teachers. As time went on, the men who became Japan's pilots were more and more poorly trained and unable to stand up against the well-trained American fliers—who also began getting planes that were equal to, and better than, the Japanese Zero fighter.

In Japan, the news of the defeat was largely withheld from the Japanese people, but it threw many of the top military leaders into deep gloom. During the months of Japanese victories before Midway, plans had been made to make more major invasions, but with the navy now crippled by the loss of those four carriers, and with the American fleet still able to give a good accounting for itself, any such invasion attempts would be far too dangerous. After six straight months of successful offense, Japan suddenly found itself on the defensive, wondering what the Americans would now do.

What the American and Allied leaders intended to do was to go on the offensive for the first time since the beginning of the war. Thus, though no one really realized it at the time, the Battle of Midway was the turning point of the war in the Pacific. From now on, things would be completely different. It would be the Americans who would aggressively take the offensive, and the Japanese who would have to defend themselves—desperately.

CHAPTER IV

AMERICA
ON THE
OFFENSIVE

The victory at Midway made it possible for American and Allied commanders to consider going on the offensive for the first time since the war had begun. They felt an attempt should be made to recapture the islands in the Solomon group that had been taken over by the Japanese in early May, resulting in the Battle of the Coral Sea. There were good reasons for retaking those islands. First, the Japanese were obviously turning them into a base from which attacks could be made on Allied ships going to and from Australia, and that was a deadly serious threat. Second, in American hands the Solomons could become bases from which to mount an attack on the important Japanese base of Rabaul, only some 700 miles (1,120 km) away. Third, there were not, as yet, many Japanese troops on them. The islands to be attacked and seized were little Florida Island and three tiny islands that lay just off Florida Island's coast: Tulagi, Gavutu, and Tanambogo. The date for their invasion was set as August 1.

But on July 4, a scout plane flying over one of the Solomon Islands called Guadalcanal made a discovery that caused the commanders to change their plans slightly. The pilot reported that there were Japanese soldiers on Guadalcanal, and that they were building an airfield. Obviously, Guadalcanal had better be included in the invasion.

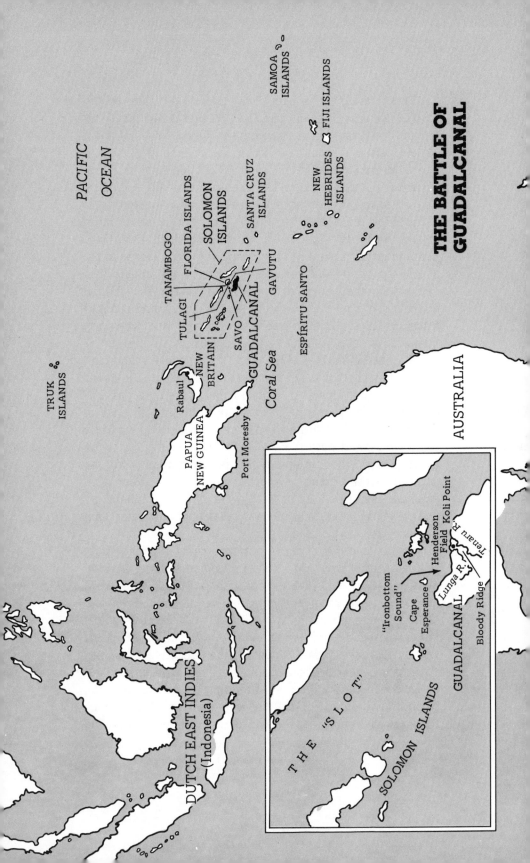

PACIFIC

OCEAN

TRUK
ISLANDS

Rabaul

NEW
BRITAIN

PAPUA
NEW GUINEA

Port Moresby

DUTCH EAST INDIES
(Indonesia)

AUSTRALIA

Coral Sea

ESPÍRITU SANTO

TANAMBOGO

FLORIDA ISLANDS

TULAGI

SOLOMON
ISLANDS

GUADALCANAL

SAVO

GAVUTU

SANTA CRUZ
ISLANDS

NEW
HEBRIDES
ISLANDS

FIJI ISLANDS

SAMOA
ISLANDS

THE "SLOT"

SOLOMON
ISLANDS

"Ironbottom
Sound"

Cape
Esperance

Henderson
Field

Koli Point

Tenaru R.

Lunga R.

GUADALCANAL

Bloody Ridge

THE BATTLE OF
GUADALCANAL

The invasion of the five islands was to be made by the First U.S. Marine Division, plus the First Marine Raider Battalion and the First Marine Parachute Battalion; a total of about 19,000 men who would be under the command of Marine Corps Major General Alexander A. Vandegrift. These marines were now training on New Zealand, and they would be carried to the islands aboard nineteen navy transport and cargo ships guarded by forty-three warships including three aircraft carriers—*Enterprise, Saratoga*, which had been patched up from damage it had received from a torpedo hit, and *Wasp*, which had been sent over from the Atlantic. The carriers and their guard of cruisers and destroyers would be commanded by Vice Admiral Fletcher, and the cargo and transport ships and their guardian warships would be commanded by Rear Admiral Richmond Turner.

Most of the marines of the First Division were young men who had enlisted shortly after the war began and had never been in combat. However, a good many of their officers, sergeants, and corporals had seen jungle fighting in Central America during a Marine Corps operation there in the early 1930s, and could pass some of their know-how along to the inexperienced men. In any event, as far as was known, the marines weren't going to encounter more than about 1,500 Japanese troops split up on Tulagi, Gavutu, and Tanambogo, and only from 3,000 to 5,000 on Guadalcanal. It seemed as if things ought to go off fairly easily.

At this time, few if any Americans knew anything about Guadalcanal or any of the other Solomon Islands. Guadalcanal is a long, fairly large island shaped somewhat like a curved baked potato. Along its middle run 8,000-foot (2,438-m) -high mountains that are mostly covered by tropical rain forest—thick, hot, wet, stinking jungle and swamp filled with birds, lizards, rats, snakes, huge crocodiles, leeches, poisonous centipedes, and hordes of flies, mosquitoes, and other insects. The jungle is a breeding ground for malaria, beriberi, and other tropical diseases—and also "jungle rot," a fungus that causes spreading sores on human skin. The island is nevertheless the home of several thousand Melanesian people, who are immune to such afflictions. The plains and hills at the feet of the mountains are covered with kunaii grass, which can be seven feet tall, is as stiff as wood, and has edges that form a row of tiny teeth like the blade of a saw. At least once a day, rain pours down.

It was to this "South Seas paradise," and to four islands much like it, that the unsuspecting Americans were headed on July 31, after the invasion force assembled in the Fiji Islands northeast of Australia. The invasion date had been pushed back to August 7, exactly eight months from the date of the Japanese attack on Pearl Harbor.

At two o'clock on the morning of August 7, the invasion ships reached Savo Island, a small cone of land sticking up out of the sea between the western tips of Guadalcanal and Florida islands. Here, the fleet split according to plan; part of it moving to the right of Savo, to take up a position off Guadalcanal, and the other part going to the left, heading for the cluster of other four islands. By 6:30 both parts of the fleet had reached their destination. The invasion began.

With thunderous crashes that shattered the silence and pierced the dim, early-morning light with bright bursts of greenish-yellow flame, the guns of the warships opened up, hurling shells in to explode among the docks and buildings the Japanese had erected on the islands. Planes from the aircraft carriers roared in low to drop bombs on selected targets and machine gun anything that moved.

Japanese seaplanes sitting in tiny Tulagi's harbor were smashed and set ablaze; the Japanese encampments on Guadalcanal were turned into a shambles, and soldiers just sitting down to a morning meal fled in panic. The Japanese had been caught completely by surprise.

The American marines assembled on the decks of the transports lying off Guadalcanal and Tulagi could see flickers and flashes of explosions on the dark masses of land and were grimly satisfied to know their enemy was being softened up so thoroughly. As the "H-Hour" landing time for each force of marines drew near, the men were ordered overboard. Cargo nets had been stretched over the sides of the ships, and the men used these as ladders, climbing carefully down them hand over hand to the landing boats waiting below, alongside the ships' hulls. As each boat was filled, the navy coxswain piloting it gunned the engine and swung his craft out in a broad curve toward the distant beach. Immediately another boat would move alongside the ship, to take on another load of fighting men.

The first landing was made on Florida Island at 7:40 A.M. The marines who splashed up onto the beach met no resistance. At eight o'clock the men of the First Marine Raiders moved onto Tulagi. The landing boats ran up against an unsuspected coral-reef barrier some distance out from the beach and got hung up, so the men had to wade ashore, starting out in water up to their armpits. They reached a beach that was blanketed with smoke from the naval bombardment and quickly moved up into the jungle. From caves, from holes in the ground, from the top of trees, Japanese soldiers opened up with rifles, machine guns, and mortars. The marines inched forward, methodically wiping out everything in their path. When they ran into resistance that was too stiff, they radioed out to the ships and soon shells came screaming in to blast the trouble spots.

At twilight, with about two thirds of the little island under their control, the marines dug in, making the shallow pits called foxholes in the earth, and waited for morning. During the night, the Japanese troops assembled in the jungle and launched wild, headlong attacks, officers waving their Samurai swords like warriors of ancient times, soldiers charging with bayonets leveled like spears and shrieking "Banzai! Banzai!" as they came. They were met with hand grenades and withering rifle fire, and after a time the attacks stopped.

In the morning the marines moved forward into rocky, hilly landscape at the southern tip of the island. Here the Japanese soldiers were holed up in caves and crevices, from which they poured deadly rifle fire into the advancing Americans. When called upon to surrender, the Japanese answered with shots and hand grenades—their intention was to die fighting. Marines crawled up to caves and threw in grenades or sticks of dynamite; crevices were cleaned out with mortars, weapons that launched single missiles high into the air so that they dropped straight down on targets, exploding when they hit. The going was slow, bitter, and bloody, but by nightfall all Japanese resistance was over and Tulagi was taken.

Four hours after the Raider battalion moved onto Tulagi, the Parachute battalion—fighting as ordinary foot troops—landed on Gavutu. They came under heavy fire as they reached the beach, and the guns of the ships were needed to pound the high ground beyond the beach where the Japanese were strongly dug in. The Americans pushed forward, and by early afternoon most of the island was under marine control.

Tanambogo is only about 500 yards (457 m) from Gavutu, and the two were joined by a long, narrow causeway—an artificial road raised above the water. The little island had been plastered by naval gunfire and battered by bombs dropped by flights of planes, but when the marines tried to move into it at six o'clock that evening they ran into a hail of fire so fierce and deadly they had to pull back onto Gavutu. It took another bombardment by the ships and an assault by an entire battalion accompanied by tanks to finally wipe out all Japanese resistance and place the island under American control.

The landing on Guadalcanal was made a little more than an hour after the one on Tulagi. The landing boats carrying the first wave of marines sped toward the island in a long ragged line, with shells from the guns of the cruisers and destroyers sailing over them to burst hundreds of yards ahead on the beach and in the jungle beyond. At ten minutes

American marines land on Guadalcanal

after nine the boats began to reach the frothing surf at the edge of the beach and dropped their flat bows open with a splash to let the marines come rushing out. The swarms of green-clad men pelted over the tan sand toward the line of tall palm trees that marked the edge of the jungle. Not a shot was fired at the Americans. The sea was dotted with more landing boats coming in behind them.

As more men, artillery pieces, vehicles, and supplies poured onto the beach, marine units slowly moved farther into the dim greenness of the jungle. The jungle was a shock to the young Americans; the heat was a thick, moist blanket that wrapped each man from head to toe and bathed him in sticky sweat, drawing the strength right out of his body. The men slogged westward, heading for a river called the Lunga. When night came they dug into the damp earth, wrapped themselves in clammy waterproof ponchos, and tried to sleep while rain poured down on them through the treetops. All night long there were frequent *cracks* of rifle fire as nervous sentries, fearing sudden attack, fired into the darkness at imagined sights or sounds.

Next day the marines reached their goal, the unfinished airfield near the Lunga, on which the Japanese had been working. Here they found an encampment from which the enemy soldiers had fled when the American naval bombardment began. The Japanese had left behind huge quantities of ammunition, gasoline, electrical and radio equipment, and tons upon tons of their major food, rice. It was beginning to turn wormy, and the young Americans sneered and poked fun at anyone who would eat such stuff.

It seemed as if the invasion had been a huge success and the Japanese were completely routed. But the Japanese did not intend to let this invasion go unopposed. When the invasion had begun on the morning of August 7, the Japanese commander on Tulagi had notified Japanese headquarters at Rabaul, and the Japanese high command at once began taking steps to turn the American invasion into a disaster.

First came a series of air raids by Japanese bombers and torpedo planes against the American ships lying in the sound, the waters between Guadalcanal and Tulagi. Two American destroyers and a transport ship were damaged.

But the next Japanese blow was far more successful. A fleet of five heavy cruisers, two light cruisers, and a destroyer was sent racing down the "Slot," which was the American nickname for the long strip of sea between the two rows of islands forming the Solomon "chain." Admiral Turner, overseeing the offloading of supplies from the transport ships, was warned by scout planes of this fleet's approach, and put a number of destroyers out to watch for its coming. But in the early morning of August 9 there was a rain squall and heavy overcast, and in the misty blackness the Japanese ships were able to creep past the watchers and catch the Allied fleet by surprise.

Seaplanes sent up from the Japanese cruisers dropped brilliant parachute flares that lit up the water revealing the Allied ships. The Japanese opened fire. The Australian cruiser *Canberra*, hit by twenty-four shells and two torpedoes, was hopelessly crippled. The American cruiser *Chicago* had most of its bow blown off by a torpedo. Shells rained down on the cruiser *Astoria*, knocking out all its guns and starting raging fires. The cruiser *Quincy* was practically blasted out of the water by gunfire and torpedoes and sank within forty-five minutes. The cruiser *Vincennes* was left burning and unable to move; it went down a short time after the *Quincy*. The destroyer *Ralph Talbot* was set afire.

By twenty minutes past two in the morning, satisfied with the tremendous damage his fleet had done, the Japanese commander ordered his ships back up the Slot. Three of them had been slightly damaged by American gunfire and thirty-seven sailors had been killed, with fifty-seven wounded. The Allies, on the other hand, ended up with four cruisers sunk, a cruiser and destroyer badly damaged, and 1,270 seamen killed and 750 wounded. It was the worst defeat ever suffered by a U.S. Navy force in a battle in all history!

And it was a serious blow to the American invasion. Earlier, Admiral Fletcher, worried about the danger of Japanese air attacks on his three precious carriers, had taken those warships farther out to sea. Now, Admiral Turner felt he no longer had enough protection for the transports. He dared not risk them, for the loss of too many would be fatal to this invasion and would cripple future invasion plans. Turner notified General Vandegrift he would have to get the transports out of the sound even though they hadn't yet finished offloading all the supplies. This meant that for a while at least, the marines on Guadalcanal and the other islands would be completely on their own, with only whatever supplies had already been put ashore, and with no planes or ships to protect them from air raids or to keep the Japanese from landing troops on the islands if they tried to do so.

By sunset on August 9, the last of the ships had left. The stretch of water between Guadalcanal and Tulagi—which the marines now called "Ironbottom Sound," because of all the sunken ships that now lay beneath it—was empty. With only enough food for about thirty-seven days, and only enough ammunition for about four days of hard fighting, should it come, the marines were now going to have to hang on as best they could, for no one knew how long.

Grimly, they went to work. They began digging in, stringing barbed wire, placing machine guns and artillery pieces, forming a big, fortified half-circle that curved from the beach into the jungle and back out again to the beach. Inside this half-circle was the airfield the Japanese had begun, and the marines now set out to finish it, because once there was an airfield on the island American planes could come to help them.

They started coming down with dysentery and jungle rot. Because it was feared their food might not last long enough they ate only two meals a day, and part of what they were given to eat was that captured, wormy Japanese rice they had sneered at. They were frequently sniped at by Japanese soldiers who had fled when the invasion began and

A marine camp in the jungle on Guadalcanal

were now living in the jungle. From time to time, marine patrols fought small battles with groups of the Japanese. And always the marines were reminded of how alone they were, when, with no American planes to chase them off, Japanese planes came arrogantly droning overhead to drop bombs on the airfield, and—with no American ships to keep them away—Japanese warships sailed confidently into Ironbottom Sound and sent shells whistling in on the Marine Corps position. The marines could only crouch in their foxholes and take it. As soon as the bombing or shelling was finished, repair crews went to work to undo the damage to the airfield.

But six days after Admiral Turner had pulled all the ships out, he managed to send a little help. Four destroyer transports sneaked in at night, bringing gasoline, ammunition, and 123 Seabees—men of a U.S. Navy Construction Battalion—to help the Marine engineers get the airfield finished. The field, which had been named Henderson Field after a Marine pilot killed in the Battle of Midway, was completed on August 18. Two days later, cheering marines watched twelve Marine dive bombers and nineteen Marine fighter planes come roaring in to become Guadalcanal's "air force"—known after a while as the "Cactus Air Force," after Guadalcanal's code name, "Cactus."

But now the Japanese high command had finally decided to do something definite about taking Guadalcanal back. In Rabaul, the job had been given to Lieutenant General Haru-kichi Hyakutake, who was the commander of the 17th Army—which included Japanese forces for the Solomons area. However, General Hyakutake did not regard Guadalcanal as much of a problem. He was under the impression there were only about 2,000 marines on Guadalcanal, and he did not think they would be able to stand up to tough, experienced Japanese soldiers anyway—after all, Japanese soldiers had easily defeated American troops in the Philippines and other places. So to retake Guadalcanal he sent a force he felt would be large enough to do the job: 1,000 skilled, veteran soldiers led by a capable, proven commander, Colonel Kiyono Ichiki.

On the same day that Henderson Field was finished, Colonel Ichiki and his men were landed on the coast of the island about eighteen miles east of the marines' fortified half-circle. They made their way along the coast to the American position and at three o'clock in the morning the day after the Marine planes had arrived, they attacked at a place where the river called the Tenaru flows out of the jungle into Iron-bottom Sound.

The attack was a sudden wild rush, the Japanese shouting and howling, throwing grenades and firing their rifles from the hip. But the marines had strung barbed wire here, and Ichiki's men piled up against it, trying to hack their way through with bayonets. The Americans opened up with everything they had: rifles, machine guns, mortars, and a 37mm artillery piece. Some of the Japanese finally got through the wire and rushed the marine foxholes, and young Americans and Japanese found themselves fighting face-to-face with bayonets and rifle butts. More marines were rushed forward to help the men in the foxholes and the Japanese were hurled back.

But Ichiki's men tried again, at once, launching another wild, shrieking charge. Once more they were pushed back. The sun rose to show the bank of the river littered with the bodies of dead Japanese soldiers.

The Japanese took up positions in a grove of coconut trees and began steady rifle and machine-gun fire. But now a Marine battalion moved into position and came at the Japanese from the flank and rear. Ichiki's men tried to break out of this closing trap with a bayonet charge, but were driven back. They began to break apart into little groups. Some charged, courageously but foolishly, and were shot down. Some climbed trees to fire down on their enemies and were killed by machine-gun fire that tore through the drooping palm leaves.

A United States plane takes off from
the newly completed Henderson Field.

By afternoon the Battle of the Tenaru River was over. The marines had lost thirty-five dead and seventy-five wounded. Nearly eight hundred Japanese were dead, fifteen captured, and the rest had managed to slip into the jungle. Colonel Ichiki, unwilling to accept what he considered the disgrace of losing a battle, committed suicide by shooting himself.

The other Japanese troops on Guadalcanal notified Rabaul, by radio, of what had happened. General Hyakutake and the other Japanese commanders acted at once to make up for Colonel Ichiki's disaster. Within a few days, a fleet of more than sixty ships was coming down the Slot, bringing 1,500 Japanese marines and veteran army troops. The fleet, which included two aircraft carriers, a light carrier and a seaplane carrier, four battleships, sixteen cruisers, thirty-four destroyers, and several other ships, was commanded by Vice Admiral Nobutake Kondo, while the carriers were under the command of Admiral Nagumo, who had commanded them at Midway. Kondo's orders were to pound the marines on Guadalcanal with bombs by day and hammer them with naval gunfire by night, and when they were softened up enough, the Japanese troops would land and finish them off. Meanwhile, if any American ships showed up, the planes of Nagumo's carriers would take care of them. The Japanese were convinced this would be the deathblow for the American force on Guadalcanal.

CHAPTER

BATTLING
IT OUT

Once again, however, the Japanese were not able to keep their movements secret any more than they had for their attempt to capture Midway. Their fleet was spotted by scout planes and coast watchers— Australians and Englishmen who were hiding out on various Japanese-held islands and keeping the Allied command informed by radio of everything they saw. Thus, the newly promoted Vice Admiral Frank Jack Fletcher, now commanding a task force of a battleship, three carriers, seven cruisers, and eighteen destroyers, cruising near the Solomons, knew the Japanese were coming. However, he now made a rather bad mistake—he didn't think the Japanese would be able to reach Guadalcanal before August 26, so he sent the carrier *Wasp* and its guard of ten destroyers off to refuel, which he felt was necessary.

But the Japanese were closing on Guadalcanal by August 24. Search planes from *Enterprise* and *Saratoga* began to report sightings of many ships. Fletcher ordered a flight of thirty bombers and ten torpedo planes launched from *Saratoga*, and these found the Japanese light carrier *Ryujo* and its escort ships. Within a few minutes *Ryujo* was hit by between four and ten bombs and one torpedo, and sank five hours later.

But even as *Ryujo* was being attacked, one of Admiral

Nagumo's scout planes discovered the two American carriers and radioed their position back to the Japanese fleet. At once, Nagumo launched eighty-one planes in two waves.

The first wave of Japanese planes found *Enterprise* at 4:30 in the afternoon. The air was filled with *Enterprise*'s fighter planes, as well as bullets and bursts of antiaircraft fire from the carrier and its nine guardian ships, but even though most of the Japanese planes were blown out of the sky, *Enterprise* was hit with three bombs that tore holes in the flight deck and started fires. However, damage control parties and repair crews worked frantically, and within an hour the fires had been extinguished and the flight deck was patched with huge pieces of sheet metal, putting the carrier back into fighting shape. Luckily for *Enterprise*, the second wave of Japanese planes never managed to find it and returned to their fleet. Night's darkness settled over the Pacific and put an end to any further air attacks.

Next morning a flight of Marine dive bombers took off from Henderson Field on Guadalcanal and went out to look for the Japanese aircraft carriers. Instead, they found the group of ships bringing the 1,500 Japanese troops to Guadalcanal. The American pilots brought their planes shrieking down and planted bombs on the light cruiser *Jintsu* and the auxiliary cruiser *Kinryu Maru*, which was full of Japanese marines. The Americans had radioed the position of these ships, and forty-five minutes later a flight of U.S. Army B-17 bombers from the distant American base on Espiritu Santo Island arrived and hit the destroyer *Mutsuki* with three bombs, sinking it almost instantly. The Japanese had now had two ships sunk and several badly damaged, many of the troops that were to have landed on Guadalcanal had been killed or injured, and so many planes had been lost in the attack on *Enterprise* that Admiral Kondo decided it was no longer possible to carry out his orders. He turned his fleet around and headed back to Rabaul. This battle, which became known as the Battle of the Eastern Solomons, was over and it was an American victory that prevented a serious

attack against the American force on Guadalcanal. Had *Wasp* been present, with all its planes available to look for the two main Japanese carriers, the victory might have been as great as the one at Midway.

The result of this battle caused a rather strange situation. The commanders of Japanese ships, now aware that the Americans could fill the sky over Guadalcanal with planes from their carriers, from Henderson Field, and even from such distant places as Espiritu Santo, became afraid to venture near Guadalcanal during daylight hours. So, American ships could finally come hurrying into Ironbottom Sound by day to bring supplies. However, they would go racing out again before sunset, because during the night Japanese ships came down the Slot to shell Guadalcanal and the American commanders did not want to be caught by them in the darkness. Thus, by day the waters around Guadalcanal belonged to the U.S. Navy, while at night they belonged to the ships of the empire of Japan.

General Hyakutake now decided to try to take advantage of this situation by sneaking troops onto Guadalcanal in small groups during the hours of darkness. From August 29 to 31, the Japanese Navy managed to land about 3,500 men with supplies, artillery, and equipment. They were under the command of a Major General Kyotake Kawaguchi, who had promised General Hyakutake that he would recapture the Guadalcanal airfield for the Japanese Empire by the beginning of October. It was probably lucky for the American marines that General Kawaguchi apparently wanted to make

*An American sailor
was killed taking this
photograph of a bomb
exploding on the flight deck
of the U.S.S.* Enterprise
on August 24, 1942.

a big name for himself, for he talked General Hyakutake out of sending in thousands of more men, insisting that he could do the job of retaking Guadalcanal with only 3,500!

Kawaguchi felt sure the Americans did not know his force was on the island, but he was wrong. The Melanesian people who lived on Guadalcanal were far friendlier to the Americans than to the Japanese, and some of them let the marines know that a large force of Japanese had taken over a coastal village called Tasimboko. General Vandegrift decided to catch the invaders by surprise, and sent the Marine Raider Battalion, six hundred strong, to deal with them.

Two navy destroyer transports landed the Raiders a short distance from Tasimboko village, and while the ships poured shells into the village, and planes from Henderson Field roared back and forth machine-gunning the area, the marines moved forward. They ran into only a small Japanese force that put up a short, fairly stiff fight, then vanished. General Kawaguchi, thinking an all-out major landing was being made against his troops, had withdrawn them into the jungle, leaving much of his supplies and even a number of artillery pieces behind in the village. The Americans destroyed all this, then returned to the ships and were taken back up the coast to the Henderson Field perimeter.

It was clear that this new Japanese force was on the island to make a major attack, so the marines began strengthening and improving their lines. General Vandegrift particularly wanted to strengthen a long ridge that stuck up out of the jungle about only a mile from Henderson Field, because it looked to him like a likely place for the Japanese to launch their main assault.

Vandegrift was right; Kawaguchi did intend to make his main attack across that ridge and head straight for the airfield. By September 12 his soldiers were massed in the jungle below the ridge. At noon that day, forty-two Japanese planes from Rabaul roared over the island on a bombing attack, and that night at precisely nine o'clock, four Japanese warships began hurling shells in at Henderson Field. The sweating marines in their foxholes, many of them half-sick with malaria and weak from only two meals a day of Spam and Japanese rice, knew the attack was coming any moment.

It burst upon the ridge a few minutes after nine; a typical "Banzai" charge! Kawaguchi's soldiers swarmed up the slope with leveled bayonets, howling. They pushed in among the marines, were beaten off, came back again. All night long the Japanese probed and pushed all along the ridge, but when morning came the ridge was still in American hands and the Japanese withdrew into the jungle, both they and the marines exhausted.

During the day there was raid after raid of Japanese bombers winging over Henderson Field. The Marine and Navy pilots roared up to meet them each time, and by the end of the day the toll was five American planes downed to eleven Japanese.

When darkness spread over the island, Kawaguchi's men attacked the ridge again, first hammering it with mortar fire, then making another screaming charge up the slope. The 105mm howitzers of the Marine artillery opened up, slamming shells into the ridge's rising slope and the jungle beyond, but the Japanese soldiers came raging right through the explosions. In places, groups of marines were pushed back, in other places they were cut off and had to fight their way to the rear through swarms of yelling Japanese. The marines pulled back, and back, and back, until they were only 1,500 yards (1,370 m) from the vital airfield, and there they formed a tight line of defense, pouring rifle and machine-gun fire, grenades, mortar shells, and 105mm howitzer shells into the oncoming Japanese at point-blank range. This was more than flesh and blood could withstand, and the Japanese fell back, came forward again, a little more weakly, pulled back again, came forward once more, more weakly still. Finally, they gave up. The Americans moved back onto the ridge. The sun rose to find the ridge perfectly quiet except for the calls of birds and hum of insects. But it was strewn with bodies. Forty marines were dead and 103

*United States marines blast Japanese
positions on Guadalcanal*

wounded, while 600 Japanese soldiers had been killed and hundreds wounded. The savage struggle that had taken place on the grass-covered slope became known as the Battle of Bloody Ridge, and though no one knew it at the time, it was actually one of the most important land battles fought during the entire war in the Pacific. For if the Japanese had broken through and captured Henderson Field, eliminating the Cactus Air Force, the marines would not have been able to keep holding the island.

During the day—September 14—there was a little more fighting as the Japanese made weak attempts to break through the Marine line in other places. But by the end of the day, General Kawaguchi's little army no longer existed. Survivors were struggling through the jungle, throwing away weapons and equipment as they went, while wounded men were flopping down to die in the hot, wet, insect-swarming underbrush.

The marines went back to their monotonous existence of heat, rain, stinging insects, malaria, and poor food. But on September 18 something happened to cheer them up a little—a navy convoy arrived with food, ammunition, some tanks, trucks, and reinforcements, in the form of the Seventh Marine Regiment, some four thousand strong.

But the U.S. Navy had paid dearly to bring these reinforcements and supplies. The aircraft carrier *Wasp*, which had been helping to guard the convoy, had been torpedoed and sunk by a Japanese submarine. With *Enterprise* and *Saratoga* (which had been hit by a torpedo on August 31) both being repaired at Pearl Harbor, there was now only one American aircraft carrier—*Hornet*—on duty in the Pacific.

However, *Wasp* hadn't died in vain; the supplies and reinforcements were going to be important. For when General Hyakutake got word of General Kawaguchi's defeat, he finally realized he had better give Guadalcanal his full attention. He now knew there were far more marines on the island than he had first thought, so he resolved to send enough soldiers to take care of them once and for all—at least 20,000.

Furthermore, he intended to come to Guadalcanal himself, to assume personal command of what he felt would be the last effort needed to retake the island.

So, on about September 20, Japanese ships began coming regularly down the Slot each night, bringing troops and then heading back to Rabaul for more. This began to seem so much like a regular boat or train service that the Americans rather bitterly dubbed it the "Tokyo Express."

As October arrived, the Tokyo Express was bringing as many as 900 well-equipped troops to Guadalcanal each night. In addition to these newcomers there were also the remains of Kawaguchi's and Ichiki's troops as well as the Japanese soldiers that had been on the island when the Americans landed. This all built up into a good-sized force, and when General Hyakutake arrived on October 9, with a large number of troops, he felt he now had everything he needed for making the major attack that would crush the Americans and recapture the island—more than 20,000 experienced soldiers, plenty of heavy artillery with which to pound the Marine position, plenty of mortars and machine guns, and even a company of tanks. He would also have plenty of help from planes based at Rabaul, and from the Japanese navy, which had provided a large fleet that was lurking near the Solomons, ready to support him with air strikes and naval gunfire.

The American commanders knew that a tremendous punch was going to be swung at the American force on Guadalcanal, and were hurrying to be ready for it. On the very day General Hyakutake landed on the island an American convoy was sent with more supplies and reinforcements for General Vandegrift. Two transports carrying food, ammunition, and 2,800 soldiers of the U.S. Army's 164th Infantry Regiment set out, accompanied by four cruisers and five destroyers under the command of Rear Admiral Norman Scott.

As these transports and warships were nearing Guadalcanal on the afternoon of October 11, Admiral Scott got word that a Japanese fleet of two cruisers and six destroyers had been sighted coming down the Slot and would reach the island by midnight. Scott had this fleet well outgunned, and he was eager to take on the Japanese in a night-fight to make up for the defeat the Americans had suffered in the night battle back on August 9. Sending the transports on by themselves, Scott turned his warships and proceeded at full speed toward the oncoming Japanese force.

The American ships encountered the Japanese a little after midnight that night, in waters near a point of land called Cape Esperance, that sticks out from the Guadalcanal coastline. In the battle that took place, now known as the Battle of Cape Esperance, the Americans sank two Japanese cruisers and a destroyer while losing only one destroyer, and drove the Japanese off. It was an American victory, but it had no real importance. The five ships Scott's force defeated were merely the ships that had been sent to bombard Guadalcanal that night, but a much larger force, sailing on a slightly different course, had gotten safely to the island and landed more troops and supplies.

Early on the morning of October 13, the two American transports arrived safely with the soldiers and supplies they carried. It was thus a cheerful morning for the Americans on Guadalcanal, but that soon changed. General Hyakutake had chosen this day to start softening up the Americans for his big offensive.

First, there were two bombing raids, with Japanese bombers droning over at noon and again at about 1:45, and severely damaging Henderson Field. Then, out in the jungle, fifteen pieces of brand-new Japanese heavy artillery opened up, and for the rest of the day shells were screaming into the American position. (The marines nicknamed these big guns "Pistol Pete.") At night, a fleet of Japanese ships, including two battleships with their enormous 14-inch (36-cm) guns, sat in Ironbottom Sound and blasted the Americans for an hour and twenty minutes. After that, more bombers came, and kept on coming off and on all night.

This went on for the next six days. The Cactus Air Force did what it could, but the bombings and naval bombardments damaged a lot of the planes and destroyed a great deal of fuel. However, by patching up lightly damaged planes with parts of badly damaged ones, and by scrounging gasoline from wrecked planes, trucks, and wherever else it could be found, the Henderson Field crews managed to get from six to a dozen or so aircraft into the sky each day to provide some challenge to the enemy aircraft.

At 12:30 in the morning of October 23, in a torrent of rain, General Hyakutake launched his big attack. Swarms of Japanese soldiers came pouring out of the jungle, screaming their "Banzai" war cry, and struck at a point half a mile south of Bloody Ridge. This point was held by men of the First Battalion of the Seventh Marine Regiment, commanded by Lieutenant Colonel Lewis "Chesty" Puller. The Marines blazed away with rifles, machine guns, mortars, and artillery fire. The Japanese pushed up to within only yards of the Marine foxholes, then dropped back, unable to move forward any farther through the hail of bullets. There was a pause, during which the young Japanese and Americans yelled insults through the darkness at each other. (Many of the Japanese spoke excellent English.) Then, Hyakutake's men came swarming forward in another wild, shrieking rush that was also beaten back.

It looked to Puller as if the Japanese were going to keep hitting with everything they had at his battalion's position until they simply wore his men down enough to break through. He didn't have enough men to hold out against such continuous attacks so he sent a message requesting reinforcements. Within half an hour, soldiers of the U.S. Army 164th Infantry were among the marines, and when the Japanese attacked again there was too much resistance for them. Each attack was a little weaker than the one before it, for after each attack there were fewer men to make the next. By dawn, the attacks came to an end, with the marines and soldiers still holding their position.

During the day "Pistol Pete" kept up a continuous shelling, and flights of Japanese bombers droned over the island again and again. When darkness fell the Japanese soldiers once more attacked near Bloody Ridge. All night long the marines and soldiers again fought off charge after charge. Farther to the west the Japanese also made three strong attacks on another part of the American position, and the third attack actually broke through. But marines from nearby positions counterattacked and finally pushed the Japanese back. Once again when morning dawned the Japanese were out in the jungle and the Americans still held the ground they had been defending all along the line. They had lost more than 300 killed and wounded, but the Japanese losses from their headlong "Banzai" charges were staggering—more than 3,500! Their insistence on sticking to their traditional, almost ancient way of fighting, and their firm belief that Americans could not stand up against this kind of fighting, had once again cost them dearly.

General Hyakutake had been completely sure that his troops would break through the American lines and capture Henderson Field before dawn on the morning of October 24, and he had sent a confident message to the Japanese fleet that the capture would take place at any moment. So the Japanese ships—four aircraft carriers, four battleships, ten cruisers, and twenty-nine destroyers—started toward Guadalcanal, to be on hand to launch air attacks that could help finish mopping up the defeated American troops.

For several days an American task force made up of the carriers *Hornet* and *Enterprise* (patched up and returned to duty), six cruisers, fourteen destroyers, and the battleship *South Dakota* had also been lying near the Solomons, under the command of Rear Admiral Thomas Kincaid. Kincaid got word from a scout plane that many Japanese ships were moving toward Guadalcanal, and shortly his task force was speeding to intercept them.

The sea battle fought on the morning of October 26 is known as the Battle of Santa Cruz, as it took place near the

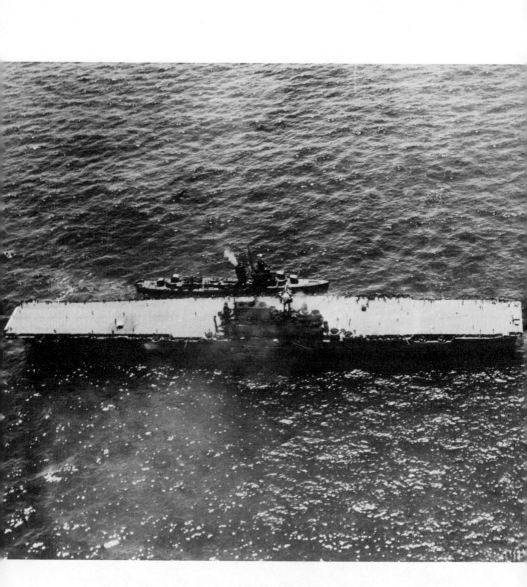

*One of the last photographs of
the U.S.S.* Hornet *before it was lost in
the Battle of Santa Cruz.*

Santa Cruz Islands, which are part of the Solomons, lying east of Guadalcanal. The battle was mainly an exchange of air attacks, with the Americans seeming to get the worst of things. The aircraft carrier *Hornet* and the destroyer *Porter* were sunk, and *Enterprise*, *South Dakota*, a cruiser, and a destroyer were damaged. The Japanese carrier *Shokaku* was so badly damaged it was out of action for nine months, and two other carriers and two destroyers were heavily damaged.

However, the main Japanese loss was in airplanes—nearly 100 were destroyed. Following the battle, the Japanese force had so few planes left that it was no longer possible to make the air attacks on Guadalcanal to help General Hyakutake. But by this time, General Hyakutake could not use any help from the navy anyway—his army was in retreat in the Guadalcanal jungle! Learning of this, the Japanese naval force left the Solomon Islands region and returned to its base in the Truk islands, some distance away.

Thus, the huge operation planned by General Hyakutake to recapture Guadalcanal simply petered out. The American troops on Guadalcanal had now stood off three attempts, each stronger than the last, to take the island away from them. And both General Vandegrift and Vice Admiral William F. Halsey, now commanding the South Pacific area forces, agreed it was now time for the Americans to go on the offensive and wipe out, capture, or drive out all the Japanese troops on the island.

There was now little doubt that they could do it, for on October 24 a decision had been made that was to be of vital importance to the war in the Pacific. In Washington, D.C., President Franklin D. Roosevelt had been listening to arguments from the top military commanders of both the Atlantic and Pacific areas of war. The admirals in charge of Atlantic operations were asking for more ships to deal with the terrible effectiveness of the German submarines that were taking a heavy toll of Allied shipping, and the generals wanted more men and planes to build up a force for an invasion of Europe some time in 1943. But Admiral Ernest J. King and General Douglas MacArthur, in charge of Pacific operations, insisted that more ships, planes, and men were needed to hold Guadalcanal and keep the Solomons as a base from which to begin launching vigorous attacks. There simply wasn't enough of everything for both the Atlantic and Pacific theaters of war, so President Roosevelt made a decision—the Pacific forces would get what they needed.

With the president's promised help, the United States forces in the South Pacific began to put together a big push of their own.

CHAPTER VI

FIRST STEP
TO VICTORY

The first few days of November bustled with activity. Navy transports brought in more marines, soldiers, Seabees, and some heavy artillery that gave the Americans on Guadalcanal a "Pistol Pete" of their own. Planes and pilots came, to rebuild the shrunken Cactus Air Force. Meanwhile, a Marine battalion was sent east along the coast toward a spot called Koli Point, where it looked as if the Japanese were beginning to mass a large number of troops together, possibly for yet another attack.

But the battalion ran into more than it could handle. The Tokyo Express had landed 1,500 soldiers at Koli Point, and the marines were thus outnumbered about three to one. The Japanese attacked with mortar and artillery fire, and the Americans had to fall back.

The battalion commander radioed for help, and General Vandegrift sent planes and reinforcements. From November 2 to November 12, the Americans and Japanese battled around Koli Point, with the Americans slowly closing a ring around the enemy force. But at the last minute the Japanese managed to slip out of the trap and vanish into the jungle. They had lost 450 men; the Americans lost 40 killed and 120 wounded.

It was clear that the Japanese high command was still sending troops to Guadalcanal and that something new was brewing. What had happened was that the Japanese had put together yet another plan for recapturing the island. They intended to pour in men and supplies throughout the months of November and December, then in January the troops on the island would attack, supported by a huge naval force that would steam into Ironbottom Sound at the same time.

On the same day that the Japanese troops slipped out of the American trap at Koli Point, a number of American cargo and transport ships, guarded by some warships, had arrived at Guadalcanal. Late in the afternoon, Admiral Turner, in command of this convoy, got word that a large Japanese fleet was approaching. He ordered all the cargo and transport ships to leave at once. Five cruisers and eight destroyers stayed behind to do their best against the Japanese.

The Japanese force consisted of two battleships, a light cruiser, and fourteen destroyers, under the command of Admiral Hiroaki Abe. They were coming to make an all-out attempt to destroy Henderson Field with shellfire, so that the Cactus Air Force could not interfere with all the Japanese troop landings that were to be made. Admiral Abe knew there were American warships in Ironbottom Sound, but he expected them to leave before sunset—as American ships had been doing since the beginning of September. His fleet moved confidently on, and by ten minutes to two o'clock on the morning of Friday, November 13, it entered Ironbottom Sound.

Suddenly, Japanese lookouts became aware of ships looming up ahead. Now began a wild, confused battle with ships plunging past one another in the darkness, bursts of gunfire ripping the night open, sudden swelling glows of red from burning vessels. At three o'clock the Japanese broke off the fighting and withdrew, with two destroyers sunk, four damaged, and the battleship *Hiei* mangled by more than eighty hits. But the little American force had been shattered. Two U.S. cruisers and four destroyers had gone to join all the other dead ships at the bottom of Ironbottom Sound. Three other cruisers and two destroyers were badly damaged.

However, the American sailors had actually won an important victory. They had kept the Japanese ships from knocking out Henderson Field. The next night the Japanese navy again tried to destroy the airfield, but this time they sent fewer ships and the commanders were in a hurry to leave, fearing another American attack. Their bombardment did hardly any damage, and when morning came the field was still operational and there were plenty of planes to take off from it. Those planes were to play an important part in the events that now took place.

First, they found the ships that had bombarded Henderson Field that night and damaged several of them with bombs. After going back to refuel and rearm, they went out again, and this time they ran into the Tokyo Express coming down the Slot with heavy reinforcements for Guadalcanal—eleven transports jammed with 10,000 Japanese soldiers and supplies and equipment.

From noon until nightfall the enemy transports were under attack. Terrified young Japanese soldiers with nowhere to run, nowhere to hide, stood and watched bombs come spinning down straight at them. Jammed together on the decks they cringed against one another as torrents of machine-gun bullets came slicing into them like deadly rain. In pain and panic they fought their way up from burning lower decks where bulkheads (walls) were beginning to glow red. As their ships shuddered from the impact of torpedoes, they leaped or were hurled into the sea until the water was thronged with bobbing heads. By the end of the day, seven of the transports were sunk or sinking and close to five thousand Japanese soldiers had perished.

As night closed over what was left of his ships, the Japanese commander, Rear Admiral Raizo Tanaka, simply decided to keep on going and land whatever troops and supplies he could. At about nine o'clock he met a group of Japanese ships on their way to making another bombardment of Henderson Field—a battleship, four cruisers, and nine destroyers, commanded by Vice Admiral Nobutake Kondo.

Tanaka's ships simply followed Kondo's into Ironbottom Sound. But there Kondo's ships found a small American task force waiting for them—two battleships and four destroyers, commanded by Rear Admiral Willis A. Lee.

The Japanese and American destroyers met head on, first, and the Americans were badly mauled. By 11:30 one was on fire and sinking, one was so badly shot up it could no longer fight and was simply trying to get away, and the other two were heavily damaged. One Japanese destroyer was badly mangled.

The battleship *South Dakota*, turning to avoid ramming the burning destroyer, blundered into the path of the Japanese battleship *Kirishima* and the two cruisers, which caught the American ship in searchlight beams and opened fire, battering it viciously. But their searchlights showed the other American battleship, *Washington*, where they were. *Washington* was a new ship, armed with big, new 16-inch (41-cm) guns that now began raining shells on the Japanese ships. *Kirishima*'s steering gear was smashed and the battleship was set afire, while the two cruisers were heavily damaged.

Admiral Kondo decided his ships were in bad trouble and ordered them all to withdraw. Lee let them go and started hunting for American survivors of the battle. As a result of the action the American destroyer *Benham* sank, but so did one Japanese destroyer and the battleship *Kirishima*. Once again, the Japanese had been prevented from knocking out Henderson Field.

While the battle was raging, Admiral Tanaka stuck right to his job and took his transports up to the Guadalcanal beach, ordering them to simply run aground, for there was no other way to get the troops and supplies onto shore. When the transports were up where the soldiers could safely begin disembarking from them, Tanaka turned his destroyers around and started back up the Slot. He had carried out his mission to land troops and supplies on Guadalcanal as best he could despite heavy air and naval assault.

However, dawn was now only a short time away, and with the morning light came American planes from Henderson Field to bomb and machine-gun Tanaka's beached transports and the men still piling out of them. The ships and supplies were totally destroyed, and of the ten thousand Japanese soldiers who had started out in Tanaka's convoy, no more than about two thousand finally managed to join General Hyakutake's ragtag army on Guadalcanal.

All this fighting that had taken place in Ironbottom Sound and the waters west of Guadalcanal from November 12 to 15 became known as the Naval Battle of Guadalcanal. Its result was: for the United States, seven destroyers and three light cruisers sunk, and for the Japanese, two battleships, a cruiser, three destroyers, and eleven transport ships destroyed. The Japanese attempt to land ten thousand men on Guadalcanal had been stopped with only one fifth of that number actually getting there; the Japanese attempts to destroy Henderson Field by naval bombardment had been thwarted.

The Japanese troops on Guadalcanal were now in bad shape. Many of the men had been living in the jungle for three months or more, without enough food and with practically no medical help. Like the American marines, thousands of the Japanese soldiers had malaria, which meant that at any time they could come down with the weakness, shivering chills, and high fever that made it almost impossible to move, much less to fight. And because of what had happened to Admiral Tanaka's transport ships, the Japanese were now also running low on ammunition. However, there was still no thought of giving up, either by the Japanese forces on Guadalcanal or by the Japanese high command. In fact, a decision was made to try again to retake the island, this time by sending an army of 50,000 men!

But in the meantime the Japanese troops already on Guadalcanal had to be kept supplied and this was no longer going to be as easy as it had been in the past. It was even impossible to sail ships up onto a beach, as Tanaka's transports had done, and let them just sit there to be offloaded—there were too many American planes and ships around these days. So Admiral Tanaka, whose job it was to keep Guadalcanal supplied, came up with the idea of filling empty oil drums with supplies, tying them together in bunches, and delivering them by means of fast destroyers that would come racing down the Slot at night and drop off the drums to let them float onto the beach where General Hyakutake's soldiers could get them.

Tanaka tried out this idea on the night of November 30, heading for Guadalcanal with eight destroyers carrying 1,100 supply-packed oil drums. However, once again there was U.S. Navy Task Force 67—six destroyers and five cruisers—lying in wait near Guadalcanal for any Japanese ships that might show up. Tanaka was caught by surprise, but he had given all his destroyer commanders orders on what to do if they encountered an enemy, and they now followed those orders. Each destroyer launched a flock of torpedoes toward the gunfire flashes of the nearest enemy ship, then immediately turned and raced away. The Americans managed to pick up one Japanese vessel on radar and battered it with a rain of shells, but then the barrage of torpedoes slammed into four of the American ships. The result of this quick battle was that the Americans traded one cruiser sunk and three others badly damaged for one enemy destroyer sunk. However, Tanaka's ships had not been able to deliver their supplies.

On December 3 Tanaka tried again. This time he didn't encounter any American ships, and his destroyers were able to drop 1,500 packed oil drums into the waters off the Guadalcanal coastline. Unfortunately for General Hyakutake's men they were able to find only 310—far from enough to do any good. Tanaka made another try on December 7, but this time his destroyers ran into planes and PT Boats, and had to turn back. It was clear that this way of delivering supplies was simply not working.

But while things were going badly for the Japanese on Guadalcanal, they were improving tremendously for the Americans. On December 9, the men of the First Marine Division, who, like the Japanese, had been living in the jungle for months without proper food or medical attention, were relieved, to regain their health in Australia. Their place was taken by fresh, healthy troops of the U.S. Army Americal and 25th Divisions. General Vandegrift went with his men, and the new commander on Guadalcanal was Major General Alexander M. Patch, U.S. Army.

Thus, when the Americans launched their big offensive on December 17, they did so with men who were in good condition and backed up with plenty of supplies, against sick, starving Japanese soldiers who were just about out of food, ammunition, and hope. They weren't out of courage, however, and the Americans often ran into stiff resistance. The Japanese pulled back slowly, fighting all the way, and it looked to the American commanders as if General Hyaku-take intended to make a last-ditch, suicidal stand at the western end of the island.

But the Americans were wrong. Actually, the Japanese high command had suddenly decided to give up on Guadalcanal. They were growing worried over American troop movements in another part of the Pacific, which seemed to be threatening Rabaul. So they had ordered General Hyakutake to fight a delaying action while he pulled his men back toward Cape Esperance on the west coast. There, ships of the Japanese navy would begin taking his men off Guadalcanal—which Japanese soldiers and sailors were now calling "Death Island."

Throughout December and January the American soldiers and new Marine units now on Guadalcanal moved in pursuit of the retreating Japanese. Meanwhile, at Rabaul, Japanese ships were assembling, and when the American commanders got word of this they decided that the Japanese were probably going to try to put reinforcements on the island again, and perhaps make a major invasion.

On the afternoon of February 1, scout planes and coast watchers reported a large number of Japanese destroyers moving swiftly down the Slot toward Guadalcanal. Is this the beginning of the big invasion? wondered the Americans. They began getting ready. Destroyers planted three

The Japanese stronghold, Rabaul Harbor,
under attack by American planes during
a raid in early November 1942

hundred mines in the waters off Cape Esperance, where it was thought the landing of troops would be made, because that was where General Hyakutake's force was now gathered. Three destroyers and eleven PT Boats moved out toward Savo Island, and the planes at Henderson Field started to warm up.

By eleven o'clock that night, twenty Japanese destroyers were nearing Cape Esperance when the PT Boats located them and attacked. But three of the boats were destroyed and not one of the many torpedoes they launched scored a hit. However, as one Japanese destroyer was turning aside to avoid a torpedo coming at it, it struck one of the floating mines and the explosion tore it open. Later, dive bombers from Henderson, searching for the enemy force in the darkness, found only the shattered destroyer, which had been abandoned and was burning fiercely. The other Japanese ships had vanished.

By morning, the Americans were sure the Japanese had managed to land a large number of troops. Actually, the destroyers had taken aboard as many of General Hyakutake's soldiers as they could, and gone racing back up the Slot.

Two days later, the Japanese came again. A cruiser and twenty-two destroyers were reported heading for Guadalcanal. Again, American PT Boats raced through the darkness in search of the enemy, but found nothing. Japanese bombers came roaring over Henderson Field off and on all night, keeping the American planes from being able to take off, and while this was going on the Japanese ships again loaded up with men and went dashing away.

The Americans were confused and worried. The soldiers and marines moving through the jungle toward Cape Esperance expected to run into heavy resistance at any moment, from fresh, well-equipped troops—but this never happened. American naval commanders had jitters as they got reports of movements of a large Japanese naval force—but this force never attacked. What was going on?

In the dark hours after midnight on February 7, eighteen

Japanese destroyers came down the Slot in a rain squall that hid their movement. These ships took aboard the last remaining Japanese soldiers, and left. Exactly six months from the day the U.S. Marines had landed on Guadalcanal, the island was finally empty of Japanese troops. The Imperial Navy had done a superb job of removing nearly twelve thousand men with the loss of only one destroyer and some damage to four others. It was one of the most clever troop withdrawals in all the history of warfare. However, even the most perfect such removal is not a victory; it is an admission of defeat. The Japanese were beaten on Guadalcanal.

The ships had barely been in time getting the last of the troops off the island, for with the coming of daylight, General Patch's soldiers and marines began moving on Cape Esperance from two directions, with the intention of catching General Hyakutake's forces between them. But two days later, when soldiers of the U.S. 132nd Infantry, coming from the west, met soldiers of the 161st Infantry moving from the east, they realized the Japanese troops they had been expecting to squeeze between them were gone.

The Guadalcanal campaign was over. The U.S. Marine and Army troops that had been on the island had lost a total of 1,598 men killed and 4,709 wounded. Japanese records for the total of their men killed, missing, and dead of wounds and disease, showed an incredible 23,800. The U.S. and Japanese navies had both had twenty-four ships sunk.

The Guadalcanal victory was not as decisive a victory as Midway—it was really just a first step on a long, long road. Nevertheless, it also represented a turning point in the Pacific war. It was the first major defeat of the Japanese Empire's previously invincible ground forces—they had been stopped dead in their steady takeover of Pacific islands. Japan's army had now joined Japan's navy on the defensive. Japan would fight on vigorously for over two more years, but it would never regain its lost momentum—it would always be fighting to *hold* what it had, and would never again be able to fight to gain something new.

A number of Japanese officers felt that Guadalcanal was

a defeat of major importance. After the war, Admiral Tanaka, the skilled commander of the Tokyo Express, remarked that "Japan's doom was sealed with the closing of the struggle for Guadalcanal." After Guadalcanal was lost, Admiral Sokichi Takagi believed that Japan should quickly try to make peace, but he dared not say so in public lest the top war leader, Premier General Hideki Tojo, should accuse him of treason.

For the American people, the Guadalcanal victory seemed much more important than the victory at Midway. Until Guadalcanal, the Japanese army had generally smashed every opponent it faced—Chinese, British, Australian, and American, and there was almost a feeling that maybe Japanese soldiers couldn't be defeated! Guadalcanal changed that. People became confident that American marines and soldiers, as well as sailors, were more than a match for the enemy. Spirits lifted, and most people now had no doubt that America would eventually win the war in the Pacific.

The Guadalcanal victory also gave confidence to American fighting men. Most of the marines who first landed on Guadalcanal had never been in combat, while most of the Japanese soldiers they faced were experienced, battle-hardened veterans. But the marines, and later the army troops, showed they could stand up to everything that was sent against them. The confidence built on Guadalcanal, and the lessons learned there, would be of help in the terrible, hard-fought battles that lay ahead.

Guadalcanal became a new American base, a very important base from which U.S. forces could move up through the Solomons toward Rabaul. Thus, it was the first step on a long path of island conquests, and it showed what was to come—American troops, supported by an ever-growing number of ships and planes, would move from island to island, wiping out the Japanese conquests, until finally only the main Japanese islands remained, to be put under steady air attack, threatened with invasion, and forced to surrender by the atom bombings of Hiroshima and Nagasaki.

FOR FURTHER READING

Blair, Clay. *Combat Patrol*. New York: Bantam Books, 1975.

Bliven Bruce, Jr. *From Pearl Harbor to Okinawa*. New York: Random House, 1960.

Braum, Saul. *The Struggle for Guadalcanal*. New York: G. P. Putnam's Sons, 1969.

Buell, Thomas B. *The Quiet Warrior*. Boston: Little, Brown and Co., 1974.

Carmichael, Thomas N. *The Ninety Days*. New York: Bernard Geis Associates, 1971.

Cook, Charles. *The Battle of Cape Esperance*. New York: Thomas Y. Crowell, 1968.

Donovan, Robert J. *PT 109, John F. Kennedy in World War II*. McGraw-Hill Book Co., New York: 1961.

Griffith, Samuel B. *The Battle for Guadalcanal*. New York: Bantam Books, 1980.

Hough, Richard. *The Battle of Midway* New York: Macmillan, 1970.

Hoyt, Edwin P. *Blue Skies and Blood*. New York: Paul S. Eriksson, 1978

Leckie, Robert. *Challenge for the Pacific*. Garden City, N.Y.: Doubleday, 1965.

_____. *Strong Men Armed*. New York: Random House, 1962.

Lee, Robert Edward. *Victory at Guadalcanal*. Noyato, Ca: Presidio Press, 1981.

McKay, Ernest A. *Carrier Strike Force*. New York: Julian Messner, 1981.

Marrin, Albert. *Victory in the Pacific*. New York: Atheneum, 1983.

Mercer, Charles. *Miracle at Midway*. New York: G. P. Putnam's Son's, 1977.

Miller, Thomas G., Jr., *The Cactus Air Force*. New York: Harper & Row, 1969.

Newcomb, Richard F. *Savo: The Incredible Naval Debacle off Guadalcanal*. New York: Holt, Rinehart & Winston, 1961.

Prange, Gordon W. *At Dawn We Slept*. New York: McGraw-Hill Book Co., 1981.

_____. *Miracle at Midway*. New York: McGraw-Hill Book Co., 1982.

Smith, William. *Midway: Turning Point of the Pacific*. New York: Thomas Y. Crowell, 1966.

Stafford, Edward P. *The Big E*. New York: Ballantine Books, 1980.

Stein, R. *Battle of Guadalcanal*. Chicago: Children's Press, 1983.

Toland, John. *But Not in Shame*. New York. Random House, 1961.

Toland, John. *The Rising Sun*. New York: Random House, 1970.

Tregaskis, Richard. *Guadalcanal Diary*. New York: Random House, 1955.

Werstein, Irving. *The Battle of Midway*. New York: Thomas Y. Crowell, 1961.

INDEX